SUPPORTING
EDMONTON'S
FOOD BANK

Flavours
of
Edmonton

DISHES FROM AROUND THE WORLD

COMPILED BY CBC EDMONTON *and* LOVONI WALKER

Lone Pine Publishing

2311 – 96 Street
Edmonton, Alberta T6N 1G3

www.lonepinepublishing.com

Library and Archives Canada Cataloguing in Publication

Flavours of Edmonton / compiled by CBC Edmonton and Lovoni Walker.

Includes index.
ISBN 978-1-55105-864-1

1. Cooking—Alberta—Edmonton. 2. Cooking, Canadian—Alberta style.
I. Walker, Lovoni, 1965–

TX715.6.F536 2011   641.597123'34   C2011-904476-5

Editorial Director: Nancy Foulds
Project Editor: Kelsey Everton
Production Manager: Gene Longson
Book Design & Layout: Janina Kürschner
Cover Design: Gerry Dotto
Cover Photo: © 2011 Thinkstock

We acknowledge the financial support of the Government of Canada through the Canada Book Fund (CBF) for our publishing activities.

PC: 5

Contents

About Edmonton's Food Bank

It's a bank that would like to go out of business but certainly not go bankrupt.

In 1981, the Edmonton Gleaners Association opened Canada's first food bank. Now, Edmonton's Food Bank (its more familiar name) is a member of the community. In one month, Edmonton's Food Bank feeds 15,000 people—40 percent of whom are children.

It takes more than 41,000 volunteer hours per year to keep this bank out of the red. And, of course, it takes many, many donations of food and money.

The sale of this *Flavours of Edmonton* cookbook will help Edmonton's Food Bank do what it does best—sustain hope by filling food hampers.

About Lovoni Walker

Born and raised in Australia, Lovoni Walker has 20 years experience in television, publishing and food consulting. She is the host of the national cooking show *Simple, Fresh, Delicious*, now on the OWN (Oprah Winfrey Network). She was one of the first food show hosts to entice people to cook food sourced locally.

She is the author of three cookbooks and co-writer of over sixty. She has been a magazine and cookbook food editor. Her recipe writing and food styling can be seen on television, in countless published works and online. She is asked to speak at conferences educating people about culinary tourism, agritourism and the local food movement. Lovoni lived in Edmonton for many years, and just recently took the position of food specialist with a Fortune 500 company.

Preface

Flavours of Edmonton is a community potluck.

In keeping with the spirit of the potluck, this collection of recipes rolls out the welcome mat. Let *Flavours of Edmonton* introduce you to the city's newcomers and to those who have called Edmonton home for years.

CBC Edmonton challenged its audience—TV, radio and online—to submit original recipes and stories. Many of those recipes became part of this collection.

We rounded out the Edmonton repertoire by approaching local restaurants to share their favourite dishes. CBC colleagues and columnists were invited to combine prose with their sweet and savory inspirations. Thanks to Isabelle Gallant and Erin Thomson Leach for their dedication gathering recipes and stories.

Thanks to NorQuest College for giving us the opportunity to meet some of their students and hear their recipes and stories firsthand.

Thanks to Lovoni Walker for spending hours in the kitchen to test each recipe.

Thanks to all those "foodies" who took the time to transcribe family favourites and share the memories behind the dishes.

Flavours of Edmonton exists because of Lone Pine Publishing, so a round of applause for their team.

And special thanks to the Edmonton Heritage Festival Association for supporting the launch of *Flavours of Edmonton* at the 2011 Heritage Festival. Proceeds from this cookbook will go to Edmonton's Food Bank.

It's the dinner table conversation and the good food that makes a meal memorable. So, whether it's a family celebration or a simple weekday supper, we hope you enjoy these recipes and stories as you sample the flavours of the world without leaving your kitchen.

Andrea Graham
Program Manager (Radio), CBC Edmonton and owner of 80-plus cookbooks

Recipe Conversions

The following equivalents can be used to convert to metric measurements.

Volume

⅛ tsp	0.5 mL
¼ tsp	1 mL
½ tsp	2 mL
¾ tsp	4 mL
1 tsp	5 mL
1½ tsp	7.5 mL
2 tsp	10 mL
1 Tbsp	15 mL
1½ Tbsp	22 mL
⅛ cup	30 mL
¼ cup	60 mL
⅓ cup	75 mL
½ cup	125 mL
⅔ cup	150 mL
¾ cup	175 mL
1 cup	250 mL
2 cups	500 mL
3 cups	750 mL
4 cups (1 quart)	1 L

Weight

1 oz	28 g
2 oz	55 g
3 oz	85 g
4 oz	115 g
5 oz	140 g
6 oz	170 g
7 oz	200 g
8 oz (½ lb)	225 g
10 oz	280 g
12 oz (¾ lb)	340 g
14 oz	396 g
16 oz (1 lb)	500 g
2 lbs	1 kg
5 lbs	2.2 kg
10 lbs	4.5 kg

Length

⅛ inch	3 mm
¼ inch	6 mm
½ inch	12 mm
¾ inch	2 cm
1 inch	2.5 cm
2 inches	5 cm
5 inches	12 cm
9 inches	23 cm
12 inches	30 cm

Oven Temperatures

200° F	95° C
250° F	120° C
300° F	150° C
325° F	160° C
350° F	175° C
375° F	190° C
400° F	205° C
425° F	220° C
450° F	230° C
475° F	245° C

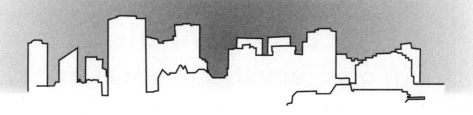

Appetizers, Snacks & Soups

Żebbuġ Mimli
(Moses' Famous Stuffed Olives)
Liz and Victor Tanti

My in-laws arrived in Canada in 1964 from Malta with four children in tow. While they loved Canada and its advantages, my father-in-law, Moses, was determined to hold onto the traditions of his homeland. There were few Maltese immigrants in Edmonton, let alone grocery stores that catered to Maltese cuisine. My father-in-law was thrilled when he learned of Frank Spinelli's Italian Centre Shop and Bakery. The family was able to find many of the foods from their homeland, and for 40 years Moses went there to pick up supplies. Initially the trips were for his own family. Later they became food runs for all his children and their growing families. Olives, a staple in Malta, were plentiful there. On special occasions he would make his famous stuffed olives, and they became a staple at celebrations as the family grew to include those of us from other nationalities.

My father-in-law died in 2000 from leukemia, leaving a large gap in our family but also a significant legacy of family, food and celebrations. His illness came on suddenly, and sadly, he died before he was able to pass on his stuffed olive recipe.

To honour his memory, my husband and I began trying to replicate Moses' Famous Stuffed Olives. We tested ingredients and interviewed my mother-in-law and other family members, including aunts and uncles in Malta. We stuffed many olives and tested them on the family. After countless adjustments and taste tests, we were successful. Now when the family comes together to celebrate, we can remember Moses/Pa/Nannu through his famous olives.

➤ 3 Tbsp chopped fresh parsley

2 tsp chopped fresh mint

2 tsp chopped fresh oregano

2 oz (58 g) tube anchovy paste
   (or 1 can anchovies, drained and mashed)

1½ Tbsp red-wine vinegar

2 slices bread, crusts removed

½ tsp cayenne pepper

2 tsp chili paste (sambal oelek)

½ tsp dried crushed chilies

5 garlic cloves, minced

2 Tbsp olive oil

2 Tbsp water

50 large pitted green olives

| **Combine** all ingredients, except for olives, in food processor. Process until smooth. Spoon mixture into piping bag fitted with plain, small nozzle. Fill each olive with mixture. Place in sealed, airtight container. Refrigerate for 24 hours before serving.

Makes 50

Mushrooms with Thyme and Ricotta on Toast

Lori Martin, Something Special Deli Foods

Something Special Deli Foods began more than 20 years ago in Sherwood Park, with two friends and a mother's secret recipe. We wanted to make antipasto to share with friends and family. We take pride in feeding the appetite of friends and family, and we love bringing people together for warmth, reunion and fabulous food. And we've spread that desire by doing what we do best—adhering to traditional artisan practices to make all of our gourmet products by hand in small batches. So, for this appetizer recipe, we relied on the expertise of Lovoni Walker to create something special.

1½ cup small, halved button mushrooms

3 Tbsp Something Special Deli Foods Jalapeño (or red pepper) dip

2 Tbsp balsamic vinegar

1 Tbsp olive oil

4 garlic cloves, minced

4 sprigs thyme

1 tsp finely grated lemon zest

pinch of salt and freshly ground pepper

4 thick slices sourdough bread

1 cup ricotta (or goat) cheese

mixed baby salad greens, to serve (optional)

Preheat oven to 400° F (205° C). Line baking sheet with parchment paper.

Combine mushrooms, dip, vinegar, olive oil, garlic, thyme, lemon zest, salt and pepper in large bowl. Spread onto prepared baking sheet. Roast in preheated oven for 12 to 15 minutes, stirring once, until mushrooms are softened.

Toast bread until golden brown. Spread warm toast with ricotta cheese and top with mushroom mixture. Serve with salad greens if desired.

Serves 4

Hearts of Fire

John Williams, Blue Plate Diner

Our goal at the Blue Plate Diner is a casual atmosphere with upscale-diner cuisine. Everything is made from scratch. Most of the dishes on our menu are the result of a collaborative process among several of our chefs. They stand around before their shift, drinking coffee and talking about the weekend specials. With all the great minds in the kitchen, ingredients come together easily to make creative dishes. Hearts of Fire is a great little zesty appetizer to serve at your next party. The spicy goat cheese plays well with the crisp, tangy, marinated artichoke hearts. After two years of having Hearts of Fire as a staple on our dinner menu, we bid them a fond farewell and offer you our recipe.

1½ cups pomegranate juice
4–6 artichokes in brine, drained
2 Tbsp olive oil
2 Tbsp lemon juice
1 garlic clove, minced
pinch of salt and freshly ground pepper

4 oz (115 g) soft goat cheese, room temperature
½ tsp chopped fresh thyme
½ tsp chopped fresh parsley
½ tsp chopped fresh basil
pinch of cayenne pepper

Boil pomegranate juice in medium saucepan for about 20 minutes until reduced to about ½ cup.

Rinse artichokes in cold water and remove chokes and any tough or brown leaves. Place artichokes in medium bowl. Add olive oil, lemon juice, garlic, salt and pepper. Toss to combine. Place artichokes, stem-end down, in medium ovenproof dish.

Place cheese, thyme, parsley, basil, cayenne pepper and pinch of salt in food processor. Pulse until smooth. Spoon mixture into piping bag fitted with plain, large nozzle, or use a sealable plastic bag. Pipe mixture into each artichoke. Broil in oven for about 3 minutes until cheese is golden. Drizzle with pomegranate reduction sauce.

Serves 4

Steamed Artichokes with Breton Cream Dressing

Juliette Champagne

When I met my future husband Yves, 22 years ago in Brittany, I purchased a small cookbook of regional Breton cooking before my return to Canada. Once home, I learned to prepare several of the typical dishes. Some regions of Brittany produce beautiful artichokes, and the little book had a variation of this recipe that included olive oil in the sauce as well as cream. We tried it, but both agreed the oil was too much. When I was growing up on a farm in Alberta, I used to make a simple salad dressing with cream and vinegar, a very traditional French recipe. It seemed to me that this is how it would have been prepared in Brittany originally. The next time I prepared the sauce I modified the recipe accordingly, using only cream, and adding fresh dill.

My now-Canadian-Breton husband loves artichokes this way, and we often begin our Saturday dinner with it. This neglected and delicious vegetable makes an impressive entrance at a dinner party or family gathering when individual serving bowls are presented en masse on a large platter. During our last trip to Brittany, we prepared artichokes in this fashion for a family dinner, and all were quite amazed, because they had never had them in this way in their region. I must add that it was great fun buying beautiful globe artichokes at the farmers' market from the producer.

> 4 large globe artichokes, trimmed
> 2 Tbsp lemon juice

Breton Cream Dressing

> 1 cup whipping cream
> 2 Tbsp white vinegar
> 1 garlic clove, minced
> 3 shallots, finely chopped
> ¼ cup chopped fresh chives
> 2 Tbsp chopped fresh parsley
> 2 Tbsp chopped fresh dill
> pinch of salt and freshly ground pepper
> 1 Tbsp drained and chopped capers
> 1 Tbsp finely chopped dill pickle

Wash and rinse artichokes in lemon juice. Put about 2 inches (5 cm) of water into bottom of large pot. Place steamer basket inside pot. Bring water to a boil. Place artichokes in steamer basket. Cook, covered, for 25 to 45 minutes (depending on size of artichokes) until outside leaves can easily be pulled off or a knife can easily be inserted into artichokes. Turn artichokes upside down to drain.

To make dressing, combine all ingredients in small saucepan over medium. Stir until warm. Serve artichokes warm with dressing.

Serves 4

Mary Tedeschini's Antipasto

Jaqui Anderson

The name Tedeschini will be familiar to many Albertans. The Tedeschinis were Italian immigrants who settled in Innisfail. Mr. Tedeschini was a shoemaker. He and his wife, Mary, had three sons. We were fortunate to be neighbours and friends with the Tedeschini family. Some of my strongest memories are of Mrs. Tedeschini, the coffee times she shared with my mother (June Scott), the homemade orange chiffon cakes she made for our birthdays and her fabulous antipasto recipe. I want to share Mary Tedeschini's Antipasto recipe to honour her and her family's contribution to our province.

1 lb (500 g) cauliflower, finely chopped

1 lb (500 g) fresh raw dills or sweet pickles, finely chopped

4 medium green peppers, seeded and finely chopped

4 medium red peppers, seeded and finely chopped

1 lb (500 g) green beans, finely chopped

1 lb (500 g) yellow (or green) beans, finely chopped

1 lb (500 g) pickling onions, peeled and quartered

4 medium carrots, finely chopped

pinch of salt

1 × 12 oz (340 mL) jar green olives, seeded and finely chopped

1 × 12 oz (340 mL) jar black olives, seeded and finely chopped

4 × 6 oz (170 g) cans white tuna, drained and broken up

4 × 10 oz (284 mL) cans mushrooms, finely chopped

1 cup white vinegar

5 cups ketchup

crackers or toast, to serve

Put cauliflower, dills, green peppers, red peppers, green beans, yellow beans, onions, carrots and salt in pot. Cover vegetables with water. Bring to a boil over high. Cook, uncovered, for about 15 minutes until vegetables are tender; drain well. Return to same pot. Add remaining ingredients. Mix well. Bring to a boil. Reduce heat to medium. Cook for about 15 minutes, stirring occasionally, until thickened slightly. Spoon into sterilized jars. Process according to canning methods.

Makes about six 2 cup (500 mL) jars

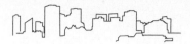

Chocolate-Covered Potato Chips

Jean Frost

This treat has been my Christmas gift to all my nieces and nephews for at least 15 years (they're now in their 20s and 30s). I learned how to make this recipe in a chocolate-making class. If you dip each chip in chocolate, you get a professional-looking product. I used to make these elegant dipped chips but decided with the volume I made, it was too time consuming. So, now it's more like an assembly line—the chips are laid out and get drizzled with chocolate. I make a cookie tin full for each niece and nephew and they know the drill: return the tin and it will be filled the next year. The tins always come back to me. The mixture of salt and chocolate works well. It's a simple yet exotic and fun snack food.

> **8 oz (250 g) sweet chocolate (Callebaut or chocolate wafers), chopped**
> **3–4 cups rippled (or plain) potato chips, approximately**

Place chocolate in medium heatproof bowl over small saucepan of simmering water. Heat until chocolate is almost melted. Remove from heat and continue stirring until completely melted.

Dip chips individually into chocolate and arrange in single layer on baking sheet until chocolate sets completely, or arrange potato chips in single layer on baking sheet and drizzle with chocolate. Allow to stand until chocolate is completely set. Store in bags or containers.

Serves 4

Croustilles au Fromage with Yogurt Garlic Dip
(Cheese Crêpe Chips)

Hans Kuhnel, The Crêperie

The Crêperie was part of the first "A Taste of Edmonton Festival" in 1984. We wanted to serve a crêpe, but the challenge was to create it away from the restaurant. So we invented this dish—deep-fried crêpe chips and dip. That first year, we didn't know how many to make because it was hard to say how popular the festival would be. We ended up selling out of crêpe chips, and they've been on our menu ever since.

This dish is popular with the high school and elementary school French classes who come on field trips to The Crêperie. It's also a favourite take-away item. One customer picks them up and brings them to his mother in Victoria as a Christmas treat. Another man who was developing a hotel in the city took home three or four orders of Croustilles every week. We hope you enjoy them too!

CRÊPE BATTER

3 large eggs
1 cup all-purpose flour
¼ tsp salt
⅔ cup water
1 Tbsp melted butter, plus extra
    for greasing pan
1 cup finely grated Parmesan cheese
vegetable oil for deep-frying

YOGURT GARLIC DIP

1 cup plain yogurt
⅓ cup sour cream
2 garlic cloves, minced
pinch of salt and freshly ground pepper
pinch of granulated sugar

Combine eggs, flour, salt, water and butter in blender. Pulse for 10 to 20 seconds until combined. Let stand for 30 minutes.

Heat large, non-stick frying pan on medium. Brush pan with a little butter. Add about ¼ cup crêpe batter and swirl to coat bottom of pan. Sprinkle with some cheese. Cook for about 1 minute until lightly golden. Carefully flip and cook for about 1 minute until golden brown. Remove to plate. Repeat with remaining batter and cheese, wiping and greasing pan in between each crêpe. Makes about 8 to 12 crêpes.

Cut each crêpe into 8 triangles. Heat oil in wok or large pot until hot. Deep-fry crêpe triangles in batches until golden brown and crisp. Remove to paper towel to drain.

To make dip, combine all ingredients in small bowl. Serve crêpe chips hot with dip.

Serves 4 to 6

Nepali Egg Curry

Kita Sitaula, NorQuest College student

This typical Nepali dish is easy and fast to cook, and has lots of flavour. This recipe is very simple, but when I cook it I often add curry leaves, bay leaves and coconut milk. I learned this recipe from my older brother. I like to cook it because it reminds me of him.

According to Narayan Pokharel, president of the Nepalese Canadian Society of Edmonton (NECASE), there are 600 people of Nepalese descent in the Edmonton area, coming from such countries as Nepal, India, Burma, Bhutan and Venezuela. NECASE volunteers do everything from organizing weekend dance and language classes to assisting newly arrived Nepalese with understanding Canadian customs and traditions. On August 15, 2010, NECASE hosted a sports event for the Nepalese communities in western Canada. In addition to football (soccer) and volleyball, the competition included Dandi Biyo—an indigenous Nepali sport that involves a two-foot-long (60 cm) wooden stick (Dandi), a six-inch-long (15 cm) wooden pin with pointed ends (Biyo), two or more players and a playing field (which can range from a small yard to an open field).

2 Tbsp vegetable oil, divided
10 hard-boiled eggs, sliced
2 medium onions, chopped
1½–2 tsp turmeric
2 tsp white vinegar

4 ripe medium tomatoes, cored and chopped
¼–½ tsp salt
½ cup chopped fresh cilantro
chapattis or rice to serve

Heat 1 Tbsp vegetable oil in large frying pan over medium-high. Add eggs in 2 batches and cook until browned. Remove from pan.

Heat 1 Tbsp vegetable oil in same pan. Add onions and cook for about 5 minutes, stirring occasionally, until softened. Add turmeric and cook for 1 minute until fragrant.

Stir in vinegar, tomatoes and salt. Cook until tomatoes are softened and wilted. Return eggs to same pan. Add cilantro and gently stir until hot and combined. Serve with chapattis or rice.

Serves 4

Jerky

Kevin Kossowan

My interest in food stemmed from multiple trips to Europe with my wife, exploring local food scenes there. I started blogging about food as a creative outlet after I stopped working in the music business. One part of my blog is a video series called "From Local Farms." I talk to Alberta farmers and producers about their jobs and their challenges.

As part of my family's effort to eat local, we hunt for our own food and butcher meat at home. I also make sausages and cured meats, like this jerky. I've made a lot of jerky: both in the oven and over wood fires, sweet-glazed versions, plain versions, smoked and unsmoked, and from various meats. This recipe is worth sharing.

1 lb (500 g) beef sirloin steak (or round steak), partially frozen

1 Tbsp salt

2 Tbsp soy sauce

2 tsp brown sugar

1 tsp freshly ground pepper

2 garlic cloves, minced

While beef is partially frozen, slice very thinly, about ⅛ inch (3 mm) thick. Try to get all slices the same thickness. Set aside.

Combine remaining ingredients in medium non-metallic bowl. Add beef and stir to combine. Cover and let sit for 24 hours if time permits.

Preheat oven to 150° F (65° C). Line baking sheet with foil. Place wire rack on baking sheet. Spray with cooking spray. Pat meat dry with paper towel. Arrange on wire rack in single layer. Cook for about 8 hours until meat is very dry and chewy (cooking time will vary depending on thickness of meat and true heat of your oven). Small pieces may have to be removed a little sooner. Let cool on rack. Place in sealed jars. Eat within 2 to 3 days. This recipe doesn't contain any preservatives, so take care when storing and only keep for a minimum time.

Serves 2 to 4

Seafood Chowder

Henry Janzen

This recipe comes from a 1974 trip to the East Coast. My good friend Peter asked me to be his best man, but it wasn't until I said yes that I learned the big day was in Nova Scotia. I spent a wonderful afternoon and evening with the bride's aunt and uncle, a captain of Canada's Icebreaker. As the aunt prepared this Seafood Chowder, I wrote down the ingredients and steps while Uncle Paul told stories and showed us Inuit art and artifacts from his travels to the Arctic. I rediscovered this piece of paper while going through my box of memorabilia. The boiled eggs are definitely unique and they bring out the distinctive flavours of the seafood.

2 large eggs

3 chicken bouillon cubes

¼ cup warm water

2 Tbsp butter

3 medium onions, chopped

¼ tsp paprika

4 large potatoes, peeled and chopped

½ tsp salt

1 quart (1 L) milk (3.25% MF)

2 × 12 oz (340 mL) cans evaporated milk

1½ lbs (680 g) chopped haddock, bones removed

4 oz (115 g) peeled and de-veined raw shrimp

6 oz (170 g) scallops, rinsed

1 lb (500 g) cooked lobster, meat removed

pinch of salt and freshly ground pepper

Cook eggs in small saucepan of simmering water for about 15 minutes until cooked. Rinse with cold water. Peel eggs and chop. Set aside.

Combine bouillon cubes and warm water in small bowl; set aside.

Melt butter in large pot over medium. Add onions. Cook for about 5 minutes, stirring occasionally, until softened. Stir in paprika. Cook for about 1 minute until fragrant. Add potatoes, salt and both milks. Bring to a boil, then reduce to a simmer. Cook, partially covered, for about 15 minutes until potatoes are almost cooked.

Stir in haddock and cook for 3 to 5 minutes. Stir in shrimp, scallops and lobster meat. Cook for 3 to 5 minutes until all seafood is just cooked and hot.

Add eggs, salt and pepper and serve.

Serves 8 to 10

Organic French Envy Soup

Elizabeth Chrapko, En Santé Organic Winery and Meadery

This unique recipe evolved one day when I was visiting our daughter, Tonia. She wanted to make onion soup and asked if I knew how to make it. I did: back in the fall of 2003, we had about 200 lbs (90 kg) of large organic sweet onions to harvest. Unexpectedly, we had a killing frost one night. We quickly pulled the sweet onions out in the morning, trimmed them, put them through a chopper and froze them in sealable bags. Following a basic recipe for French onion soup became an efficient way to salvage our crop.

But the recipe that I gave Tonia called for ingredients that she did not have, so we experimented. She did not have white wine; however, she did have a bottle of our Green Envy Alfalfa wine in the fridge. We used that and the soup turned out fantastic—with requests for seconds!

> **3 Tbsp organic butter**
> **3 medium organic onions, chopped**
> **2 bay leaves**
> **½ cup organic Green Envy wine by En Santé**
>   **(or white wine of your choice)**
> **1 quart (1 L) organic beef broth**
>   **(or chicken or vegetable broth)**
> **pinch of salt and freshly ground pepper**
> **croutons to serve (optional)**
> **finely grated fresh Parmesan cheese to serve (optional)**

Melt butter in large pot over medium-high. Add onions and cook for about 15 minutes, stirring occasionally, until softened and golden.

Add bay leaves and wine. Reduce heat to medium-low. Simmer, uncovered, for about 5 minutes until almost all wine is evaporated.

Add broth, salt and pepper. Cook, covered, for about 15 minutes until onions are very soft. Remove bay leaves before serving. Serve individual portions topped with croutons and cheese if desired.

Serves 4 to 6

Bob's Southwestern Soup

Bob Campbell

One of the cornerstones of my wife's diet used to be a bland, listless soup that she stoically ate almost every day for lunch. The cabbage- and onion-based mélange, whose rendering and digestion both filled our home with an unsavoury aroma, brought to mind the brew concocted in the opening act of Macbeth. Although nutritionally sound, it was tragically lacking in flavour and appeal. Born of a need for zest, colour and less cabbage, Bob's Southwestern Soup was created.

The theme of this soup was shamelessly stolen from a couple of television cooking shows, eliminating that which did not fit the mould of a calorie-reduced recipe, and adding vegetables, some more vegetables and finally topping it off with a few vegetables. The general idea is chicken soup donning some boots and a ten-gallon hat and heading south of the border—with some vegetables.

This soup is a combination of smoky undertones and bright tangy flavours. A number of the ingredients can be substituted with your personal favourites. The heat can be dialled up or down by adding or limiting chipotles and chili peppers. Anyone desiring a heartier version can add cornmeal to thicken things up. Vegetables are optional. You can buy roasted peppers in a jar or from the deli section in most grocery stores, or you can roast them yourself.

CHICKEN STOCK
➤ **1 × 3 lb (1.5 kg) whole chicken, rinsed**
1 large onion, halved
1 garlic bulb, halved crosswise

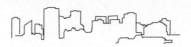

Soup

➤ **1 Tbsp olive oil**

1 medium onion, chopped

2 garlic cloves, minced

1 Tbsp ground cumin

½ tsp fennel seeds

1 × 14 oz (398 mL) can diced tomatoes, with juice

4 roasted peppers, chopped

3 canned (or dried) chipotle peppers, chopped

2 jalapeño peppers, chopped

2 cups chopped celery

2 cups chopped carrot

pinch of salt and freshly ground pepper

2 cups chopped zucchini

2 cups chopped green beans

To make chicken stock, put chicken, onion and garlic in large pot. Add enough water to completely cover chicken. Bring to a boil and reduce heat to medium. Simmer, partially covered, for 2 hours. Drain and reserve stock. Remove chicken from bones, chop and set aside. Discard skin and bones.

To make soup, heat olive oil in pot or large saucepan over medium-high. Add onion and cook for about 5 minutes until softened. Add garlic, cumin and fennel and cook for about 1 minute until fragrant.

Add tomatoes, roasted peppers, chipotle peppers and jalapeño peppers. Stir in celery, carrot, salt and pepper. Add reserved stock. Cook, covered, for about 20 minutes until vegetables are cooked.

Add zucchini, beans and reserved chicken. Cook, covered, for 5 to 10 minutes until beans are tender.

Serves 6

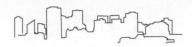

Kadhi
(Buttermilk Soup, or How to Claim Your Gujarati Roots in 15 Minutes)

Usha Joshi

My family comes from the state of Gujarat in India, where Gujaratis pride themselves on their culinary repertoire. Most of the traditional recipes demand a lot of planning, soaking and grinding of ingredients, patient simmering of foods and a lot of stirring of liquids to stop them from boiling over.

Kadhi is a favourite soup that can be included in a feast or simple supper. It is one of the handful of dishes that are unique to Gujarat (hence the reference your Gujarati roots). I have shared this modified recipe at bridal showers and with career couples, students and anyone who likes shortcuts to great food.

This soup makes an excellent accompaniment for rice dishes or any kind of bread. It is also a low-calorie, creamy, tangy comfort food in the winter. Many a lost voice has been found after a couple of bowls of hot Kadhi!

You can get fresh curry leaves at Indian grocery stores.

3 Tbsp chickpea flour (besan or gram flour)
2 cups buttermilk (or 2 cups full-fat yogurt)
2 cups water, divided
¾ tsp salt
½ tsp turmeric
1 Tbsp ghee (or vegetable oil)
1 tsp finely grated fresh ginger
1 tsp dried crushed chilies

¼ tsp ground cumin
¼ tsp black mustard seeds
3 whole cloves
1 cinnamon stick
6 curry leaves
1 Tbsp finely chopped fresh cilantro
pinch of asafoetida (optional)

Combine chickpea flour, buttermilk, 1 cup water, salt and turmeric in medium saucepan over medium. Whisk until thickened.

Heat ghee in large saucepan over medium-high. Add ginger, chilies, cumin, mustard seeds, cloves and cinnamon stick. Cook for 1 minute3, stirring, until fragrant.

Stir in 1 cup water and chickpea flour mixture. Add remaining ingredients. Cook, uncovered, over low for about 10 minutes until soup is hot and curry leaves have infused soup. Remove curry leaves, cloves and cinnamon stick before serving.

Serves 4

Lorenne's Tomato Soup

Portia Clark, CBC Television

This is a recipe my mom, Lorenne, used to make at least once or twice a summer when the tomatoes were fresh. We would help with the chopping when we were old enough, and all enjoy that big pot of soup for days! It's so good that you can even eat it cold, although I prefer it hot. I made it a lot during my university days, albeit usually with not-so-ripe tomatoes. When my brother and I were travelling after graduation, we made it in Turkey because we could get all the ingredients easily except for cooked ham. So we experimented and discovered that substituting canned tuna is also quite tasty.

Serve with crusty bread on the side, a dollop of yogurt or sour cream on top, and chopped chives or fresh basil. Nice with a slice of cheese or grated cheese, too.

> 1 Tbsp olive oil
> 2 medium onions, finely chopped
> 5 celery stalks, finely chopped
> 8 oz (225 g) cooked ham, chopped
> 1 × 6 oz (170 g) can tomato paste
> 5 medium potatoes, peeled and finely chopped
> 8 ripe medium tomatoes, cored and chopped
> 2 Tbsp chopped fresh oregano
> 2 quarts (2 L) chicken broth (or vegetable broth)
> pinch of salt and freshly ground pepper

Heat oil in pot over medium-high. Add onions and celery. Cook for about 5 minutes, stirring occasionally, until softened.

Add remaining ingredients. Bring to a boil. Reduce heat to medium-low. Cook, partially covered, for 20 to 25 minutes until potatoes are cooked.

Serves 8

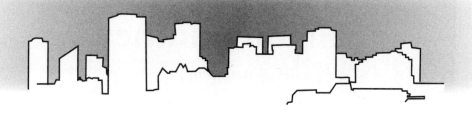

Sides & Salads

Salmon Chutney

Shiela Appavoo

My family is Indian, via Mauritius and South Africa, so I'm not certain of the exact ethnic origin of this recipe. I haven't seen it in an Indian restaurant or cookbook, so I suspect there's a bit of a local South African and/or Mauritian influence.

I thought it was quite a Canadian recipe, too, using a typically Canadian main ingredient—salmon. Salmon Chutney is usually served on rice, but it's delicious in a sandwich, particularly on thick-cut brown bread. If the bread is slightly stale, that's all the better because the juices soak into the bread. One of my favorite memories is my mother handing me a foil-wrapped Salmon Chutney sandwich on a long road trip. The bread would be falling apart and I'd have to keep it partly wrapped in the foil so that it wouldn't end up on my lap or, worse, the back seat of the family car!

2 Tbsp canola oil

8 fresh curry leaves (optional)

1 small onion, chopped

2 jalapeño peppers, chopped

4 medium tomatoes, chopped

1 Tbsp tomato paste

4 garlic cloves, minced

1 tsp finely grated ginger

¼ tsp granulated sugar

pinch of salt and freshly ground pepper

2 × 7.5 oz (213 g) cans red or pink salmon, drained, bones removed and flaked

1 Tbsp chopped fresh cilantro

Heat canola oil in large saucepan over medium-high. Add curry leaves, onion and jalapeño peppers. Cook for about 5 minutes until onion and peppers are softened.

Add tomatoes, tomato paste, garlic, ginger, sugar, salt and pepper. Cook for 5 to 10 minutes, stirring occasionally, until tomatoes are cooked.

Stir in salmon. Cook for 10 to 15 minutes, stirring occasionally, until thickened. Add cilantro.

Serves 4

Ripe Tomato Catsup

Donna Southworth

This recipe has been in my maternal family for at least three generations. The recipe probably came with the family from Ontario, but I've never been able to discover its true origins. As a young girl, I often came home from school to the telltale smell of spices filling our home, which I can't say agreed with my nose. Yet the cooking aroma didn't lessen my use of the catsup. I loved its distinctive taste on cold roast beef, fish and scrambled eggs. The cinnamon, cloves and ginger really come through.

As an adult, when my garden produces lots of tomatoes, I double the recipe.

After all these years, I've encountered this homemade catsup only once elsewhere, and it was during a trip to Newfoundland. It was part of a relish table at a fish supper. I was immediately excited when I recognized the familiar taste and assumed I was about to solve this recipe puzzle. But the "catsup contributor" was nowhere in sight and, even after queries, could not be found.

1½ lbs (680 g) ripe vine-ripened tomatoes	1 tsp ground cinnamon
2 medium onions, chopped	1 tsp ground ginger
1 cup granulated sugar	¼ tsp ground cloves
¾ cup white vinegar	1 Tbsp salt

Make small X in bottom of each tomato. Carefully place half of tomatoes in boiling water in large saucepan. Boil for about 2 minutes until skin starts to peel away. Remove to large bowl of cold water. Repeat with remaining tomatoes. Peel tomatoes and remove cores. Chop tomatoes coarsely.

Combine tomatoes and remaining ingredients in pot or large saucepan. Bring to a boil and reduce heat to medium. Simmer for about 20 minutes, stirring occasionally, until mixture has thickened and reduced.

Spoon mixture into sterilized canning jars. Process according to canning methods. Let cool; store in cool, dark place.

Makes about six 1 cup (250 mL) jars

Transylvanian Sauerkraut

Victor Dorian

My family has been making versions of this 17th-century Transylvanian dish for generations. This particular version is something of an amalgamation of the sauerkrauts my mother and grandmother used to make. My grandmother was an amazing cook, always whipping things up from scratch in our kitchen and passing along traditional recipes to my mother.

Historically, Transylvania was at the crossroads of many different cultures. You'll see culinary influences from nearby countries like Austria and Hungary in a lot of Transylvanian cuisine. Now that I have my own family in Canada, we like to add in elements from other cultures. That's the neat thing about living in Canada—you can take pieces of different traditions and make them into something completely new.

I think this recipe will stand the test of time because it's basic, good old-fashioned comfort food. Cabbage and ground meat—it's integral to Transylvanian cuisine. My two teenage sons are both starting to get interested in cooking and I was delighted to teach them how to make this dish.

K & K Foodliner has a great selection of sauerkraut.

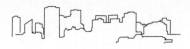

- 2 Hungarian smoked sausages (or Chorizo), sliced
- 2 quarts (2 L) wine sauerkraut
- 2 Tbsp butter, divided
- 1 cup uncooked rice
- 2 cups low-sodium beef broth

- 2 medium onions, finely chopped
- 1½ lbs (680 g) ground pork
- 1 Tbsp Hungarian paprika
- 1 cup sour cream
- 5 oz (140 g) prosciutto (or bacon)

Preheat oven to 350° F (175° C). Grease large casserole dish.

Heat large frying pan over medium. Cook sausage for about 5 minutes to remove excess fat. Set aside on paper towel to drain.

In pot over medium-high, heat sauerkraut with some of its juice for about 10 minutes, stirring occasionally. Drain well.

Melt 1 Tbsp butter in medium saucepan over medium. Add rice and stir to coat. Add broth. Cook, covered, for about 15 minutes until tender. Fluff with fork; set aside.

Melt 1 Tbsp butter in large frying pan over medium-high. Add onions and cook for about 5 minutes, stirring occasionally, until softened. Add pork. Cook for about 10 minutes, stirring and breaking up any large lumps, until browned. Stir in paprika.

Layer one-third of sauerkraut in prepared dish. Spread half of rice over sauerkraut. Spread half of pork mixture over rice. Add one-third of sausage. Cover with half of sour cream. Repeat with another third of sauerkraut, remaining rice, remaining pork, another one-third of sausage and half of prosciutto. Cover with remaining sauerkraut, sausage and prosciutto. Spread with remaining sour cream. Bake, covered, in preheated oven for 45 to 60 minutes until hot.

Serves 12

Curried Cauliflower

Amanda Schmaltz

This recipe features one of my favourite vegetables with a sophisticated, flavourful spin. I have to give the credit for this dish to my mom. She often makes it and I love it. She's my cooking inspiration. She can make a meal out of whatever she happens to find in the fridge or pantry, and she taught me how to cook at a young age.

Now, food has become my life's work. I'm a dietetic intern so food and cooking is at the heart of my job. I believe in a moderation philosophy. I think it's important to eat food to nourish your body, but also to enjoy it!

As Thomas Edison once stated, "The doctor of the future will give no medicine but will interest his patients in the care of the human frame, in diet, and in the cause and prevention of disease...The physician of tomorrow will be the nutritionist of today." That quote always resonates with me, both at work and in the kitchen.

> **3 Tbsp white vinegar**
> **3 Tbsp canola oil**
> **2 Tbsp granulated sugar**
> **2 Tbsp dry white wine**
> **2 tsp curry powder**
> **1 tsp salt**
> **1 garlic clove, minced**
> **4 cups cauliflower florets**

Combine vinegar, canola oil, sugar, wine, curry powder, salt and garlic in large bowl; set aside.

Blanch cauliflower in large pot of boiling salted water for 2 to 3 minutes until tender but still crisp; drain. Place cauliflower in large bowl of ice water. Let stand for 5 to 10 minutes to cool completely; drain well.

Add cauliflower to vinegar mixture and toss to coat.

Serves 8

Bacon Nachynka

Cindy Lazarenko, Culina Family Restaurants

Nachynka is a traditional Ukrainian cornmeal casserole. I remember eating it as a child, and we still prepare it at the restaurant today. It's a very simple recipe, but it's so comforting I think I could eat it every day. My dad used to make this when we were kids—in fact, it's the only thing he made. My mom usually did all the cooking. She made more tedious recipes like perogies and cabbage rolls. Then my Dad would whip this up in about ten minutes and get all the attention. Everyone was so excited for Nachynka.

➤ **¼ cup butter**
¼ cup bacon fat
1 medium onion, chopped
2 cups cornmeal
1½ tsp salt
½ tsp freshly ground pepper
1 quart (1 L) boiling water
2 large eggs
2 cups milk
½ tsp dried crushed chilies
⅛ tsp vanilla (optional)

Melt butter and bacon fat in large saucepan over medium-high. Add onion and cook for about 5 minutes, stirring occasionally, until softened. Reduce heat to medium.

Add cornmeal, salt and pepper and cook for 3 minutes, stirring constantly, until well coated in butter mixture; do not brown. Add water, ½ cup at a time, stirring constantly.

Whisk eggs and milk in small bowl. Add to cornmeal mixture a little at a time, stirring constantly. Remove from heat.

Stir in chilies and vanilla, if desired. Serve immediately.

Serves 6

Vegetable Caviar

Aza Dobrusina, NorQuest College student

This is a lovely food from my childhood. I remember my mom making it all the time. When I grew up I began to cook it. My family always remembers the nice taste of the Vegetable Caviar my mother cooked, so I try to cook it the way my mother did. Now I cook it every week.

➤ **1 medium eggplant**
1 medium onion, chopped
1 medium red (or green) pepper, seeded and chopped
2 ripe medium tomatoes, cored and chopped
1 Tbsp vegetable oil
pinch of salt
pinch of granulated sugar

Preheat oven to 400° F (205° C). With skewer or fork, pierce eggplant in several places. Place eggplant on baking sheet. Roast, uncovered, in preheated oven for 45 to 60 minutes until browned and skin is blistered.

Let eggplant stand until cool enough to handle. Slice open and scrape out flesh into food processor. Discard skin.

Add remaining ingredients. Blend until finely chopped. Scrape into medium saucepan. Bring to a boil over medium-high. Reduce heat to medium-low. Cook, covered, for 15 to 20 minutes, stirring occasionally, until tomatoes are broken down and mixture is cooked.

Serves 4

Yorkshire Pudding

Sean O'Farrell

Grandma Kehoe was born at the end of the 19th century in Newfoundland to parents of Irish descent. Her cooking prowess lived on through her daughters' mastery in the kitchen, making corned beef, cabbage and the old standby at family get-togethers: roast beef, mashed potatoes and, of course, Yorkshire Pudding.

The taste and texture of these large oversized Yorkies is marvellous and their appearance is extraordinarily unique. My mother and her sisters made these every Sunday that the family got together, and they always made them in smaller muffin tins. It was at my niece's wedding a few years ago that I learned that Grandma Kehoe made them in large round cake pans. I thought I would try to make them the same way Grandma Kehoe did. So with the help of my girlfriend, Laurel Anne, who supplied her very own Gramma's cake pans all the way from Ireland, we baked the Yorkies the very same way Grandma Kehoe did when she was raising her children in Redhead Cove, Newfoundland.

These amazing Yorkies can be cut into wedges for people to share, smothered in gravy and mashed potatoes, or left whole and used as an edible plate stuffed with delicious leftovers.

1 cup all-purpose flour
1 tsp salt
2 large eggs

1 cup milk (3.25% MF)
¼ cup fat reserved from roast (or vegetable oil)

Preheat oven to 425° F (220° C).

Place flour, salt, eggs and milk in blender. Blend until smooth. Cover and chill batter for 30 minutes.

Divide reserved fat between four 8-inch (20 cm) cake pans. Place pans in preheated oven for 5 minutes until fat is hot. Working quickly, divide batter between pans. Bake for 15 to 20 minutes until puffed and golden. Serve immediately with roast beef.

Makes 4

Preserved Egg Congee
Yonghua Wen

One day, a friend invited my family to her house for a barbecue dinner. We brought some food with us and went to my friend's home. When we arrived, we talked about how to make some soft food. I decided to cook congee with preserved egg, knowing it would be delicious. Congee is a soupy-style rice dish. I tried following a recipe to cook congee but ended up adding more water than usual. I didn't worry since there was a lot of food to eat. After taking 40 minutes to prepare the congee, we sat down to eat. After a meal of beef, shrimp, mushroom, chicken and so on, we moved to the congee. Even though we were almost full at this point, many of us had two bowls. The pot was emptied—it was that good.

Preserved eggs can be found in Asian markets and specialty stores.

2 quarts (2 L) water (or chicken broth)
1 Tbsp soy sauce
1 cup uncooked long-grain white rice
¼ tsp salt
¼ tsp seasoned salt

½ cup chopped preserved egg
½ cup chopped cooked chicken
1 Tbsp finely grated fresh ginger
1 bunch green onions, chopped
1 tsp sesame oil

| **Combine** water, soy sauce, rice, salt and seasoned salt in large pot. Bring to a boil. Reduce heat to medium. Cook, uncovered, for 20 to 30 minutes, stirring occasionally, until rice is very tender and mixture has thickened. Stir in remaining ingredients and serve.

Serves 4

Okra Rice

Douti Fadiga, NorQuest College student

Okra Rice is common to the Malinké people in West African countries. There are many varieties. Day to day we eat it without fish or meat, but for special events like weddings, birthdays, baptisms or funerals, we make it with chicken. It is my family's favourite dish.

➤ 3 lemons

2 tsp powdered prawn (or dried shrimp, ground) (optional)

pinch of salt and freshly ground pepper

2 Tbsp vegetable oil

10 chicken thighs (or one whole chicken, cut up)

2 medium onions, chopped

2 sprigs thyme

2 medium ripe tomatoes, cored and chopped

2 cups chicken broth

¼ cup whipping cream

3 Tbsp butter

OKRA RICE

➤ 2 Tbsp butter

2 medium carrots, peeled and chopped

2¼ cups uncooked long-grain white rice

1 quart (1 L) water

2 small eggplant, chopped

6 okras

| **Juice** lemons and strain into medium non-metallic bowl. Add powdered prawn, salt and pepper. Add chicken and stir to combine. Marinate in refrigerator for 1 hour if time permits.

Heat vegetable oil in pot over medium. In 2 or 3 batches, cook chicken for about 5 minutes until browned. Remove from pan. Add onions and cook for about 5 minutes, stirring occasionally, until onions are softened. Return chicken to pan. Add thyme, tomatoes and broth. Bring to a boil. Reduce heat to medium-low. Cook, covered, for about 45 minutes, stirring occasionally, until chicken is cooked and no longer pink. Stir in cream and butter. Remove from heat. Remove thyme sprigs.

To make rice, melt butter in large saucepan or pot over medium-high. Add remaining ingredients. Bring to a boil. Reduce heat to low. Cook, covered, for 30 to 35 minutes until vegetables and rice are tender. Fluff with fork. Serve rice with chicken.

Serves 6 to 8

Noodle Pudding

Gail Hall, Seasoned Solutions

This recipe was a family favourite growing up in my Jewish home in Toronto. It brings back memories of family dinners, celebrations and happy times.

For a savoury noodle pudding, omit the raisins, apple and cinnamon, and add chopped parsley. You can also add leftover cooked meats, chopped finely, or sautéed vegetables, and turn this dish into a casserole entrée.

My favourite ricotta is Franco's. It's locally made in Calgary and available at the Italian Centre. You can get locally made butter from Johnson's Family Farm, one of the vendors at the Salisbury Farmers' Market on Thursdays between 4 and 8:30 pm. Choose free run and/or organic eggs if you can. BC Apples from Steve and Dan's booth at the Strathcona Farmers' Market or City Market on 104 Street are some of the best I've ever tasted.

8 oz (225 g) egg noodles
2 Tbsp butter
1 cup ricotta cheese (or cottage cheese)
½ cup sour cream (or yogurt)
2 large eggs

½ cup raisins
1 cup grated apple
pinch of salt
¼–½ tsp ground cinnamon

Heat oven to 350° F (175° C). Grease and line 5 × 9 inch (12 × 23 cm) loaf pan.

Cook noodles in large pot of salted, boiling water for 6 to 8 minutes until *al dente*; drain. Rinse noodles with warm water; drain well. Return to same pot. Add butter and stir to coat.

Combine ricotta, sour cream and eggs in medium bowl.

Add raisins, apple, ricotta mixture and salt to pasta. Stir to combine. Spoon into prepared pan. Sprinkle with cinnamon. Bake in preheated oven for about 30 minutes until edges are golden brown. Let stand in pan for 5 minutes before cutting into slices. Serve warm.

Serves 8

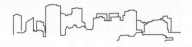

Kuppershnuck
(Sauerkraut "Soup")

Twyla Campbell, CBC Edmonton AM restaurant reviewer

My ancestors, Volga Germans, came to Canada in 1899. They, along with thousands of other Eastern European immigrants, settled in the southeastern corner of Saskatchewan. Recipes were rarely written down and followed exactly. Instead, dishes were created from memory and made with a little bit of *this* and a little bit of *that*. Kapusniak (sauerkraut or cabbage soup) was a common dish favoured by Ukrainian and Polish settlers. My grandmothers, mother and aunts made a similar dish, but instead of using potatoes and carrots as called for in kapusniak, they used rice, and pronounced the dish *Kuppershnuck*. It is not so much a soup, but more a casserole and makes a wonderful side dish with roast chicken or pot roast. My family has never had a written record of this recipe until now, and it comes courtesy of my aunt in Roblin, Manitoba, who we lovingly refer to as the Queen of Kuppershnuck.

➤ 1 lb (500 g) bacon, chopped

1 Tbsp olive oil

1 medium onion, chopped

2 garlic cloves, minced (optional)

2 cups (1 × 500 mL jar) sauerkraut, drained

1 cup uncooked long-grain rice

2½ cups chicken broth or water, approximately

pinch of salt and freshly ground pepper

Heat large frying pan over medium-high. Add bacon. Cook for about 5 minutes until golden. Drain fat and discard. Remove bacon to large pot or Dutch oven.

Heat olive oil in same frying pan. Add onion and garlic. Cook for about 5 minutes, stirring occasionally, until onion is softened. Add to bacon.

Add remaining ingredients to bacon mixture; stir. Bring to a boil. Reduce heat to very low. Cook, covered, for 40 to 50 minutes until rice is tender and mixture is thickened (the mixture should resemble that of a stew).

Serves 6

Quinoa Salad

Wilson Wu, Wild Tangerine

Quinoa Salad was inspired by the concept of "eating for benefits," which I learned about while attending SIAL (an international trade show for the food industry) in 2006 in Paris. I was very excited to win a fellowship and sponsorship to attend. During the site visits and lectures, I discovered how eating for benefits was becoming a mainstream approach in European food markets. Consumers were demanding "super food" such as berries, grains and seeds. The benefits included boosting energy and improving health. At that time, I was introduced to many seeds—including quinoa.

Try serving Quinoa Salad with a purée-based vegetable or squash soup poured around the salad, or with cooked halibut on top.

> **12 oz (340 g) quinoa**
> **½ cup finely chopped seeded cucumber**
> **¼ cup finely chopped onion**
> **½ cup finely chopped red pepper**
> **1 jalapeño pepper, finely chopped**
> **¼ cup finely chopped green onion**
> **2 garlic cloves, minced**
> **1½ Tbsp lemon juice**
> **1 Tbsp lime juice**
> **pinch of salt and freshly ground pepper**
> **¼ cup olive oil**
> **1 cup diced firm tofu**

Place quinoa in fine metal sieve. Rinse under cold running water until water runs clear. Put quinoa in medium saucepan and add enough water to fill halfway. Bring to a boil and cook, uncovered, for 10 to 15 minutes until tender; drain. Rinse under cold water; drain well. Place in large bowl. Add remaining ingredients. Toss gently to combine. Serve cold.

Serves 6

Cheesy Mashed Potatoes

Marion Broverman

When my kids were young, we lived in the neighbourhood of Riverdale, or what was known in the 1980s as "down in the flats." In those days, Riverdale was made up of many cultures and our friends taught me quite a bit about cooking. I loved to try new recipes, spices, herbs and other cultural foods with my children. This way I could make sure they learned to *try* everything. What they liked or disliked was their decision to make. I also always experimented with ingredients to make something economical that went far. Potatoes were always a good plan.

My mother and grandmother gave me my love for cooking and their teachings helped me become the cook I am today. I've graduated from a catering program with a retirement dream of running a bed and breakfast. My daughter loves to cook as well, and she now shares the recipes she learned from me and my sister with her 15-month-old.

8 large potatoes, peeled and quartered
1 medium onion, peeled and chopped
1 garlic clove, minced (optional)
pinch of salt

¾ cup sour cream (or plain yogurt)
½ cup softened cream cheese
¼ cup melted butter
1 cup grated Cheddar cheese, divided

Preheat oven to 350° F (175° C). Grease shallow 2 quart (2 L) casserole dish.

Place potatoes, onion and garlic in large saucepan. Add salt. Cover with water. Bring to a boil. Reduce to medium-high. Simmer, uncovered, for about 20 minutes until tender; drain. Mash until no lumps remain. Add sour cream, cream cheese, butter and ½ cup Cheddar cheese. Stir to combine.

Spoon potato mixture into prepared dish. Smooth top. Sprinkle with ½ cup Cheddar cheese. Cover and chill for 1 hour.

Bake in preheated oven, uncovered, for 35 to 45 minutes until hot and golden brown on top.

Serves 8

Best Bean Salad

Gloria Strathern

My love of cooking came from my mother. She always had a garden and canned her bounty for winter. I can't recall her ever buying even a single vegetable. Everything she served was from scratch so our family enjoyed homemade noodles and bread. When I think back now, I can't believe the amount of work she did.

Her efforts inspired me. Not everything in my house is homemade, and we do go out on Fridays for an end-of-the-week meal, but making something from scratch is still a mainstay at our house. And I take some pride in discovering a recipe I can share with my mother.

I first tasted this salad 30 years ago. My best friend invited me to her family's reunion at an acreage just outside of Edmonton. There was a lot of great food but this salad hit my taste buds just right and I loved it. It turns out it was my best friend's mother who brought the recipe, so getting a copy was in the cards.

When I served it to my mother at our next family event, she loved it and wanted the recipe. So I in turn shared it with her. Since then it has been shared with other family members including my sister and sister-in-law. We all fondly call it Cori's Mum's Best Bean Salad and it has become a classic in our homes.

My mother still has a garden, so she will add her own twist to the salad (yellow and green beans) whereas I prefer chickpeas. When I make this salad, I'm reminded of the fun and excitement of sharing recipes and dishes with family and friends.

Dressing

- ½ cup canola oil
- ½ cup white-wine vinegar
- ⅓ cup granulated sugar
- ¼ cup chopped fresh parsley
- ½ tsp tarragon
- ½ tsp basil
- ½ tsp dry mustard
- ½ tsp salt

Salad

- 1 × 14 oz (398 mL) can kidney beans, rinsed and drained
- 1 × 14 oz (398 mL) can yellow beans, rinsed and drained
- 1 × 14 oz (398 mL) can green beans, rinsed and drained
- 1 × 14 oz (398 mL) can chickpeas, rinsed and drained
- 1 medium onion, finely chopped

Add all dressing ingredients to jar with screw-top lid. Shake well to combine.

Combine all remaining ingredients in large bowl. Drizzle with dressing and toss to combine. Cover and marinate in refrigerator for 8 hours or overnight.

Serves 8

Sister-in-Law Salad

Peggi Ferguson-Pell

I wish I could hate my sister-in-law. I suppose in a darker moment I could tell you she's like her salad—very green, nutty, cheesy and some kind of fruit—but the truth is she's very attractive, incredibly talented and to make it all even worse, she's a genuinely nice person. Did I mention she's also a terrific cook? Grrrrrrr. Still, it does mean I am the lucky recipient of some terrific recipes.

We received this recipe as a straight swap for my husband's famous homemade hot chocolate sauce. Back in the 1970s, my husband and I turned to the chocolate sauce as very small consolation for our souls whenever Scotland crashed out of the World Cup (which was always). But that's another story for another day… that and eating curried haggis washed down with copious amounts of whiskey… don't ask. In any case, my sister-in-law loved the sauce and we loved the salad, so it was a fair exchange.

You know, now that I come to think of it, my sister-in-law knows just about nothing about the World Cup. Well, nobody's perfect!

DRESSING
- ⅓ cup olive oil
- 2 Tbsp balsamic vinegar
- 1 Tbsp Dijon mustard
- 1 Tbsp honey

SALAD
- 6 cups mixed baby lettuce leaves
- ⅓ cup pecans, toasted
- 4 oz (115 g) blue (or goat) cheese, crumbled
- 2 medium ripe pears, peeled, cored and chopped
- pinch of salt and freshly ground pepper

| **Add** all dressing ingredients to jar with screw-top lid. Shake to combine.

Toss all remaining ingredients in large salad bowl. Drizzle with dressing. Toss gently to coat.

Serves 4 to 6

Salad Olivier

Natalia Bukhanova

A Russian proverb says, "A house is beautiful not because of its corners, but because of its meals."

Salad Olivier is also known as Russian Salad or Winter Salad. This salad, which can be as filling as a main meal, is very popular in Russia and all around the world.

There are at least two versions of the origins of this salad. According to one of them, it was invented by a French cook, Lucien Olivier, who was the owner of a famous St. Petersburg restaurant in the 19th century. As the story goes, the recipe was very complicated and a guarded secret, which Olivier took to the grave. About 50 years later, the recipe was restored.

According to the second story, Russian Salad was well known for hundreds of years as a base for a summer cold soup called *Okroshka*. Nowadays, specialists believe that the modern Olivier is the mix of this traditional base and the salad created by the French chef.

2 medium potatoes, peeled
1 medium carrot, peeled
2 large eggs
1 small white onion, finely chopped
8 oz (225 g) ham (or bologna), finely chopped

6 medium dill pickles, finely chopped
1 × 14 oz (398 mL) can green peas, drained
½ tsp salt
½ cup whole egg mayonnaise
2 Tbsp chopped fresh dill

Boil potatoes and carrot until just cooked; cool. Finely chop. Place in medium bowl; set aside.

Cook eggs in boiling water in small saucepan for 10 to 12 minutes. Drain and refresh under cold water. Peel and chop; set aside.

Add remaining ingredients except dill to potatoes and carrot. Toss gently to combine. Arrange on serving plate. Sprinkle with egg and dill.

Serves 4

Beet Vinaigrette Salad

Orysia Wozniak, Taste of Ukraine

I grew up in Edmonton, the daughter of immigrant parents from Ukraine. My husband (George, a.k.a. Yuriy) also grew up in Edmonton, the son of immigrant parents from Ukraine. We shared a similar childhood. Both of our mothers were actively involved in the Ukrainian community. Their love of the Ukrainian kitchen influenced both of us in our formative years and it was just a natural progression to start a restaurant as a tribute to our ancestry. We opened Taste of Ukraine in 2004. Our son, our daughter and now our daughter's husband are involved in the restaurant. Once a week we all roll up our sleeves and cook together. It is reassuring to know that they are taking such an avid interest in carrying on the traditions.

The most beloved of Ukrainian festivities is the Holy Christmas Eve Supper (*Svyata Vecherya*). Twelve meatless Lenten dishes are prepared, symbolic of the twelve Apostles. Beet Vinaigrette Salad is served as a cold appetizer accompanying pickled herring and jellied fish *studynetz*. This salad is also served widely in all regions of Ukraine throughout the year. It has earned respect from our Canadian customers at Taste of Ukraine for its nutritional value. It is a popular low-calorie menu item, especially appreciated by customers with special dietary needs such as celiac disease.

1½ cups navy beans
4 cups cooked, peeled and diced beets
  (about 8 beets)
1 medium red onion, finely minced

½ cup diced dill pickles
⅓ cup white vinegar
¼ cup vegetable oil
pinch of salt and freshly ground pepper

Place beans in medium bowl. Cover with water. Soak overnight; drain. Place beans in large saucepan. Cover with water. Bring to a boil. Reduce heat to medium. Cook beans, uncovered, for 45 to 60 minutes until tender; drain. Rinse under cold water; drain well. Set aside.

Combine beans and remaining ingredients in large bowl. Cover and refrigerate for 30 minutes before serving.

Serves 8

Fattoush Salad

Riad Ghazal, Co Co Di

My wife and I are from Lebanon and came to Canada in 1990. In 2000, we opened our Edmonton restaurant, Co Co Di. At Co Co Di, we use mostly family recipes, like this Fattoush Salad. Fattoush Salad was invented in Lebanon early in the 20th century. A women in a small town was known to be a little bit crazy. One day, she noticed her bread was stale, so she fried it up. She took tomatoes and cucumbers, a little bit of this, a little bit of that, and threw it all together. She mixed it up, added lemon juice and olive oil, and called it Fattoush: a combination of many things coming together as one.

Farfahin, or purslane, is a fresh herb similar to mint. You can buy it in Middle Eastern or Lebanese grocery stores.

1 pita bread (brushed with olive oil)
2 cups chopped romaine lettuce
½ green pepper, chopped
½ red pepper, chopped
½ yellow or orange pepper, chopped
1 medium vine-ripened tomato, chopped
½ English cucumber, chopped
2 radishes, thinly sliced
2 Tbsp chopped fresh parsley
2 Tbsp chopped red onion

2 Tbsp pomegranate seeds
2 Tbsp Farfahin leaves (optional)
1 Tbsp fresh mint leaves

DRESSING

⅓ cup olive oil
3 Tbsp lemon juice
½ tsp dried mint (optional)
pinch of salt

Preheat oven to 350° F (175° C). Place bread on baking sheet. Bake for 10 to 12 minutes until golden and crisp. Let cool, then break into pieces; set aside. Combine lettuce, green pepper, red pepper, yellow pepper, tomato, cucumber, radishes, parsley, onion, pomegranate, Farfahin leaves and mint leaves in large bowl.

Add all dressing ingredients to jar with screw-top lid. Shake to combine. Drizzle vegetables with dressing. Add pita bread and toss just before serving.

Serves 4

Pineapple Cheese Salad

Valerie Smith

This recipe comes from my grandmother, Grandma Delisle, who probably first served it in the 1930s. I've been making it for years now and consider it the most fabulous salad. It's great for a special meal such as Christmas dinner, but it's definitely not for calorie counters.

Pearl, my grandmother, was born in Fonda, Iowa, in 1891. Her mother died when she was 10 years old, and since she was the only girl in the family, cooking for her father and her three brothers fell to her.

Pearl and her father came to Canada and settled near Saskatoon, in the area that became known as Delisle, Saskatchewan. It was named after her second husband, Ed Delisle, and his three brothers. Eventually Pearl and Ed and their two daughters moved to Alberta, finally settling in Edmonton. Grandma Delisle lived a long life—she died six months short of her 102nd birthday. She was a classy lady and a wonderful cook and hostess.

½ cup cold water
2 packets gelatin (about 2 Tbsp)
1 cup pineapple juice
3 Tbsp lemon juice

¾ cup granulated sugar
1 cup whipping cream
2 cups diced canned pineapple, with juice
1 cup grated sharp Cheddar cheese

Place water in medium microwave-safe dish. Sprinkle gelatin over water. Let stand for 2 minutes. Microwave on 50% power for 2 to 5 minutes (times will vary depending on wattage of your microwave) until gelatin is dissolved. Stir in pineapple juice, lemon juice and sugar. Cover and chill for about 2 hours until partially set.

Beat cream in medium bowl until soft peaks form. Fold cream, pineapple and cheese into gelatin mixture. Spread into mould of your choice. Cover and chill for 4 hours or overnight until set. Carefully turn onto serving plate to serve.

Serves 8

Pickled Beet Potato Salad

Gina McArthur

This salad is a staple dish in a Newfoundland cold plate supper. I grew up just knowing how to make it—although I'm sure either my mother or grandmother taught me. On Sunday, the noontime meal is usually a "boiled dinner"—potatoes, carrots, turnips and cabbage are boiled with salted beef or pork and served with a roast. For supper that night, the leftover potatoes are made into a variety of salads, like this one, and then served with the leftover cold meat, coleslaw, tomatoes and lettuce.

My husband was in the military, so we moved across the country with our two boys. This salad remained a favourite in our home. We moved to Morinville in 2005 and when our family came west for visits, this salad was served up. I've also served it to my Alberta friends, who just raved about it. Beets seem to be popular here because there's such a strong Ukrainian influence.

My husband has retired now, and we are moving back to Newfoundland to reunite our boys with their extended family. In a sense, this recipe is coming home, but I'm happy to share it with other Edmonton families.

> **6 large potatoes, peeled and quartered**
> **1 cup sliced and drained pickled beets**
> **1 small onion, chopped**
> **½–¾ cup salad dressing (such as Miracle Whip)**
> **pinch of salt and freshly ground pepper**

In large saucepan on medium-high, cook potatoes in salted water until tender. Drain well. Return to saucepan and coarsely mash.

In small bowl, mash beets with fork until coarsely mashed. Add to potatoes. Add remaining ingredients and stir to combine. Spoon into serving bowl. Cover and refrigerate for 8 hours or overnight.

Serves 8

Salad Dressing

Iris Loewen

My mom is from Switzerland. We didn't like the commercial salad dressings here and couldn't find any Swiss ones, so she made her own. When I was around 12, the job of making salad dressing passed to me. Only one of my three kids likes salad with dressing, but he always requests this one and sometimes helps me make it, too. You can make variations easily by changing the type of oil and using mayo or yogurt, different types of mustard and different herbs. A small change can make the whole salad different.

This dressing is good for a cucumber or tomato salad, or for our favourite salad: lettuce, cukes, tomatoes, red/yellow/orange peppers and butter leaf lettuce.

3 Tbsp canola (or safflower) oil

1 Tbsp whipping cream

1 tsp sour cream

1 tsp prepared mustard

1 tsp salad dressing (such as Miracle Whip)

2 Tbsp apple-cider vinegar

¼ tsp seasoned salt

¼ tsp dried tarragon

¼ tsp basil

¼ tsp oregano

¼ tsp dill

¼ tsp savory

Place all ingredients in jar with screw-top lid. Shake well to combine. Refrigerate until ready to use.

Makes about ½ cup

The Salad Everybody Loves

Nola Keeler, CBC Edmonton

This is a modification of a salad that a friend in Whitehorse told me about. She used purple onions and walnuts, but I found the onions a bit too tart and my children didn't like them. I've always liked fruit in salads and so decided to try apple instead. And how can you go wrong with pecans? I knew this salad was a big hit when even my dad—who generally avoids green leafy vegetables like the plague—asked for a second helping. Every time I serve this salad, I'm asked for the recipe. So here it is!

> ¼ cup olive oil
> ¾ cup pecans
> pinch of salt
> 4 cups baby lettuce leaves
>   (or salad green of your choice), approximately
> 2 apples, cored and thinly sliced

BALSAMIC VINAIGRETTE
> 2 Tbsp balsamic vinegar
> 1 tsp granulated sugar
> pinch of salt and freshly ground pepper

Heat olive oil in medium frying pan over medium. Add pecans. Cook for about 5 minutes, stirring regularly, until toasted. Remove pecans to paper towel; cool. Chop pecans coarsely. Pour oil into jar with screw-top lid and set aside.

Toss pecans, salt, lettuce and apples in medium salad bowl.

Add all balsamic vinaigrette ingredients to oil in jar. Shake well to combine. Drizzle over salad and toss to coat.

Serves 4

Seafood Yum

Susan Mounma, Viphalay Laos and Thai Restaurant

Seafood Yum is a sort of salad that makes a great summer dish. It's fresh and light but still has a ton of kick to it. It also very nicely represents the balance of flavours that are so important in Thai cooking: sweet, sour, salty and spicy. You can tell that a Thai dish is made well if you can taste each of the flavours without one overpowering another.

4 small squids, cleaned
8 large raw shrimp, peeled and de-veined
12 large scallops, rinsed
8 mussels
pinch of salt

SALAD

2 shallots, thinly sliced
2 Tbsp finely chopped lemongrass
1 cup cashews, toasted
2 green onions, sliced
1 celery stalk, thinly sliced (Chinese celery adds extra flavour)

1 large ripe Roma tomato, cut into thin wedges
1 Tbsp pickled garlic juice (optional)
2 Tbsp chopped fresh cilantro

DRESSING

3 small red Thai chili peppers, finely chopped
4 Tbsp fish sauce
4 Tbsp lime juice
1 Tbsp grated palm sugar (or brown sugar)
3 garlic cloves, minced
1 tsp finely chopped cilantro stalks
3 cloves pickled garlic, minced

Cut squid open, score (cut small slits) inside and cut into 2 inch (5 cm) pieces. Place ½ inch (12 mm) water in large saucepan. Add all seafood and salt. Cover and cook for 2 to 3 minutes until seafood is just cooked. Drain and set aside.

Toss seafood together with all salad ingredients.

Put all dressing ingredients in blender or food processor. Blend or process until well combined. Pour over salad and toss gently to coat.

Serves 4

Main Dishes

Culina's Grilled Sirloin with Blue Cheese Cream and Red Wine Chocolate Sauce

Peter Brown, CBC Radio's Radio Active

I've sent dozens of people to Culina Mill Creek to try Brad Lazarenko's signature dish, and without exception the verdict has come back "amazing." It's a leap of faith for some people, though—it doesn't sound like it should work. You don't think of blue cheese and steak going together, or blue cheese and chocolate, but the blend of flavours and textures, the tanginess of the cheese and the sweetness of the chocolate, creates a combination that's absolutely winning.

The story behind the dish is equally surprising. Six or seven years ago, before he opened Culina, Brad was visiting the home of Dianna Funnell, who now runs Bibo, the winebar next to Culina. She had laid out some snacks—nuts, olives, blue cheese and dark chocolate. They started talking about how well the chocolate went with red wine, and also how well the cheese and wine went together. In other words, Brad says, it began as a fluke. From there he started experimenting, and since then this hard-to-describe dish has scored points for me with many friends and visiting relatives.

4 × 9 oz (255 g) beef sirloin steaks
potatoes, cooked and mashed, to serve

Blue Cheese Cream

3 Tbsp butter
2 Tbsp finely chopped onion
1 tsp minced garlic
¼ cup dry white wine
1 cup whipping cream
⅓ cup creamy blue cheese
salt and freshly ground pepper to taste

Chocolate Sauce

1 cup demi glaze
¼ cup red wine
pinch of salt
½ tsp freshly ground pepper
3 Tbsp grated dark chocolate

Grill steaks over medium-high until cooked to your likeness. Cover and set aside.

To make blue cheese cream, heat butter in medium frying pan over medium. Add onion and garlic. Cook for about 5 minutes, stirring occasionally, until softened. Add wine and simmer until wine is reduced by about half. Add cream and cook until thickened. Stir in blue cheese, salt and pepper. Simmer for 5 minutes. Keep warm.

To make chocolate sauce, combine demi glaze, wine, salt and pepper in medium frying pan over medium. Simmer for 5 minutes to cook alcohol off wine. Remove from heat. Add chocolate and stir to combine.

To serve, place steaks on mashed potatoes. Drizzle with blue cheese cream and chocolate sauce.

Serves 4

Pirata Sueco
(Meatball Tortillas)

Mario Cerna

I was born in Monterrey, Nuevo León, Mexico, but moved to Edmonton in 2007 with my wife and children. The Pirata is a large wheat tortilla taco that is very popular in the northeast of Mexico. I was in high school when I first tried this taco and I recall being very impressed because it was both tasty and fulfilling. Traditionally it has grilled beef or pork, cheese and avocado. In Mexico, I would make it for my wife on special occasions or when we wanted to indulge ourselves. Since moving to Canada, I use Swedish meatballs because, like Mexican grilled meat cuts, they have a strong beef flavour. Different cultures enrich each other.

> **1 Tbsp olive (or vegetable) oil**
> **½ large onion, diced**
> **1 large whole-wheat tortilla**
> **10 small meatballs (preferably Swedish),**
>   **sliced and warmed**
> **⅓ cup grated mozzarella (or asadero) cheese**
> **1 small avocado, mashed**
> **2 Tbsp chopped fresh cilantro**
> **pickled jalapeño peppers to serve (optional)**

Heat olive oil in large frying pan over medium-high. Add onion and cook, stirring occasionally, for about 10 minutes until golden. Remove from pan and set aside; wipe pan clean.

Place tortilla in same pan over medium. Add meatballs, cheese and onion over half of tortilla. Fold other half over to cover meatballs. Cook for 3 to 5 minutes per side until golden brown.

Remove tortilla to serving plate. Spread with avocado. Sprinkle with cilantro. Serve with jalapeño peppers if desired.

Serves 2

Beef Rouladen

Gloria Strathern

This is an old German recipe. Every year on a birthday, Mom would ask the birthday child to pick their favourite for dinner. We always asked for "crumbsy meat" as we called it. We loved these tender rolls, and all the tasty morsels that would find their way into the gravy, all the crumbs! This brings back all those wonderful childhood memories of home-cooked food made by our mom, and dinners spent together around the table, with Dad telling us great stories from the old country.

2 lbs (1 kg) beef sirloin

¼ cup Dijon (or prepared) mustard, divided

¾ cup finely chopped pickles, divided

¾ cup finely chopped onion, divided

¾ cup finely chopped bacon, divided

¾ cup all-purpose flour, divided

pinch of salt and freshly ground pepper

2 Tbsp canola oil

2½ cups beef broth, divided

mashed or roasted potatoes for serving (optional)

Preheat oven to 325° F (160° C). Grease medium ovenproof baking dish.

Pound beef until about ¼ inch (6 mm) thick. Cut into strips about 3 inches (8 cm) wide. Spread mustard on top of each slice. Divide pickles, onion and bacon between each slice. Roll up slices to enclose filling. Secure with toothpicks. Combine ½ cup flour, salt and pepper in shallow dish. Dredge each roll in flour. Lightly shake off excess.

Heat canola oil in large frying pan over medium-high. Cook rolls in batches until browned. Transfer to prepared baking dish. Add 1½ cups broth; cover with foil. Cook in preheated oven for about 1 hour until cooked. Remove rolls and keep warm. Reserve pan juices.

Heat pan juices over medium-high. Add ¼ cup flour. Whisk to remove any lumps. Gradually whisk in 1 cup broth. Add salt and pepper. Cook for about 5 minutes until thickened. Strain to remove any lumps. Serve with beef rolls and potatoes if desired.

Serves 8

Tamale Pie

Pat Lore

Sundays for me always mean Sunday Supper, held on a loosely rotating schedule at the home of some lucky family member. Tonight it's my turn, and the 21 guests (by no means an unusual number) represent three generations of extended family, with an assortment of in-laws (and maybe a couple of outlaws) thrown in for good measure. On the menu: Tamale Pie. It's always a hit—classic comfort food, a recipe my mom got from the Texas wife of an oil patch co-worker of my dad's in the 1950s. Some of the young'uns mash it all together with ketchup. Others load on the hot sauce. I know the recipe doesn't look like much, but every time I make it for my Sunday Supper, the reaction is the same: "Tamale Pie? I was hoping you would make it!"

No one needs to tell me how lucky I am. My grown children eat with all four grandparents almost every week. Nine of my parents' twelve grandchildren live here in Edmonton, and the cousins are closer than many siblings. There is no fourth generation yet, but we're all looking forward to it—a highchair is just what Sunday Supper has been missing!

Tamale Pie is easy to double (or triple!) for a crowd, and the leftovers can be sent home with hungry relatives.

1 Tbsp vegetable oil

1 large onion, chopped

1½ lbs (680 g) ground beef

1 cup water

½ cup cornmeal

1 tsp salt

¼ tsp freshly ground pepper

1 × 14 oz (398 mL) can corn kernels

2 Tbsp chili powder

1 × 28 oz (796 mL) can diced tomatoes,
   with juice

CORNMEAL TOPPING

2¼ cups milk

2 Tbsp butter

¾ cup cornmeal

3 large eggs, lightly beaten

1½ cups grated Cheddar cheese

¾ tsp salt

Preheat oven to 375° F (190° C). Grease medium-large casserole dish.

Heat vegetable oil in large frying pan over medium-high. Add onion. Cook for about 5 minutes until softened. Transfer to large saucepan.

Add beef to same frying pan. Cook for 10 to 15 minutes until browned; drain fat. Add beef to onion.

Add water, cornmeal, salt, pepper, corn, chili pepper and tomatoes to beef mixture. Cook over medium for about 10 minutes, stirring, until thickened. Spread into prepared dish.

To make cornmeal topping, heat milk and butter in medium saucepan over medium. Stir in cornmeal. Cook, stirring, until mixture is thickened. Add eggs one at a time. Add cheese and salt and stir until cheese is melted. Spread over beef mixture. Bake in preheated oven for 35 to 40 minutes until topping is cooked and golden.

Serves 6

Babote
(Baked Meat)

Koleal Scott

My mother introduced this recipe to our family (four kids and a Norwegian father) over 50 years ago and we have recently rediscovered it. We were intrigued because she told us the recipe was African. Looking back, I think this recipe was a bold move in a household that was accustomed to roast beef and meatloaf for dinner. I asked Mum where she got the recipe and she can't recall (she is now 93 years old). I believe this recipe introduced us to curry, which we all love today. Now my grandkids are learning to love Babote!

4 Tbsp butter, chopped, divided
2 medium onions, finely chopped
2 Tbsp medium curry powder
1 egg, lightly beaten
1¼ cups milk
1 lb (500 g) lean ground beef
1 cup fine dried breadcrumbs

½ cup dried apricots (or raisins), finely chopped
1 Tbsp granulated sugar
1 tsp salt
steamed rice, to serve (optional)
chutney, to serve (optional)

Preheat oven to 375° F (190° C). Grease medium casserole dish.

Melt 2 Tbsp of butter in medium frying pan over medium-high. Add onions and cook for 5 minutes until softened. Add curry and cook for 1 minute until fragrant.

Beat egg and milk together in small bowl.

Combine beef, onion mixture, egg mixture and remaining ingredients in large bowl. The mixture at this stage will be quite wet. Spoon into prepared dish. Smooth top.

Scatter 2 Tbsp butter over top of casserole. Bake, uncovered, in preheated oven for about 45 minutes until golden. Serve with rice and chutney if desired.

Serves 4 to 6

Chabli Kabob

Abdul Fatah Kohistani, NorQuest College student

I was living in Russia when I tasted this kabob for the first time. It was my friend's original recipe. He owned a restaurant in Russia that was very popular and always crowded. I taught myself how to make it so I could share it. I arrived in Canada ten months ago with my wife and daughter. Now when I cook this recipe in Edmonton for friends and family, it reminds me of my friends from all over the world.

2 medium onions, finely chopped

8 garlic cloves, minced

2 tsp garam masala

1 tsp paprika

1 tsp salt

1 lb (500 g) lean (or regular) ground beef

2 large eggs, lightly beaten

1 Tbsp all-purpose flour

2 Tbsp vegetable oil

rice, potatoes or pasta to serve (optional)

Combine onions, garlic, garam masala, paprika and salt in large bowl.

Add beef, eggs and flour and mix well to combine. Shape mixture into 12 small patties.

Heat vegetable oil in large frying pan over medium. Cook patties in batches until cooked through. Serve with rice, potatoes or pasta if desired.

Serves 4

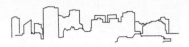

The Barsby Shepherd's Pie

Stephanie Barsby, CBC Edmonton meteorologist

This was a common dinner in the Barsby household. My grandma would make it for my mum's family, then my mum would make it for us three kids, and now I make it for my two kids. Since time is tight right now, this variation of the classic English "cottage pie" does the trick for me. Unlike the traditional dish, which is baked in the oven for at least half an hour (and that's on top of the prep time), I can get the Barsby version from kitchen to table in about 30 minutes. And coming from television, I know it is true—every minute does count.

2 lbs (1 kg) potatoes, peeled and quartered

⅔ cup milk (3.25% MF)

2 Tbsp butter

pinch of salt and freshly ground pepper

1 Tbsp vegetable oil

1 medium onion, chopped

1 lb (500 g) ground beef

1 Tbsp all-purpose flour

⅔ cup beef broth

¼ cup ketchup

¼ cup tomato paste

2 Tbsp Worcestershire sauce

pinch of salt and freshly ground pepper

1 medium ripe tomato, sliced

1 cup grated Cheddar cheese

2 Tbsp finely grated fresh Parmesan cheese

Grease casserole dish. In large saucepan of salted water, cook potatoes over medium for about 20 minutes until tender. Drain and mash until no lumps remain. Stir in milk, butter, salt and pepper; set aside.

Heat vegetable oil in large frying pan over medium-high. Add onion and cook for about 5 minutes, stirring occasionally, until softened. Add beef and cook for 10 minutes until browned. Stir in flour and cook for 1 minute. Add broth, ketchup, tomato paste, Worcestershire sauce, salt and pepper. Stir to combine. Cook, uncovered, for 5 to 10 minutes, stirring occasionally, until thickened. Spoon into prepared dish. Spread mashed potatoes over top. Arrange tomato slices over top. Sprinkle with both cheeses. Broil for about 5 minutes until golden.

Serves 4 to 6

Mush

Felice Young

The idea for this recipe came on a day I felt creative and wanted a different twist to the usual hamburger-type recipes. It has since become a family favourite, with its great flavour and a lingering, tantalizing aroma that leaves you with a warm and fuzzy feeling. It's easy and fast to make (takes about a half hour), inexpensive and best served on a cold day. If you want to add a little spice, add a small amount of Matouk's hot pepper sauce (available at any store that sells Middle Eastern food—I get mine at Spice Island in West Edmonton Mall). It's very hot, but very flavourful.

You will need to cook a cup of rice for this recipe. This recipe is perfect served on toasted hot buns.

1 Tbsp olive oil
1 cup finely chopped onion
¾ cup finely chopped celery
¾ cup finely chopped red pepper
6 garlic cloves, minced
1 lb (500 g) ground bison (or beef)
1 Tbsp basil
1 Tbsp oregano

1 tsp salt (or to taste)
1 tsp freshly ground pepper (or to taste)
1 tsp Mrs. Dash (optional)
2 cups frozen corn, thawed
2 × 10 oz (284 mL) cans cream of
   mushroom soup
3 cups cooked fragrant rice

Heat oliv e oil in large frying pan over medium-high. Add onion, celery, red pepper and garlic. Cook for about 5 minutes, stirring occasionally, until softened.

Add bison. Cook for about 10 minutes, stirring occasionally and breaking up any large lumps, until cooked.

Add remaining ingredients and cook for about 10 minutes, stirring occasionally, until hot.

Serves 6 to 8

Côm Bō Lúc Lác
(Beef Tenderloin with Fragrant Rice)

Eileen Jang, Phởbulous

My husband Jimmy and I are part owners of the Vietnamese restaurant Phởbulous. Jimmy emigrated from China to Alberta with his family as a child, settling in Fairview, a town north of Grande Prairie. His parents ran a restaurant there, and Jimmy was only in his teens when his father died. He was forced to take over the family business.

At first he was resentful, because he had bigger dreams: to go to university and find a new career. But as the years went on, he realized how much he loved the restaurant business. He became very successful, and he knew that this tragedy early in life had been a great opportunity.

I am a dentist and have my own practice. Jimmy and I were married 13 years ago, and he moved from Fairview to Edmonton so we could be together. I was worried about Jimmy since he had to sell his restaurants in Fairview and Grande Prairie. We were the landlords for the building where Phởbulous now is, and when it opened three years ago, the founders proposed that we become part owners. It was the perfect plan: now Jimmy has a place to hang his hat in Edmonton.

Jimmy maintains that running a restaurant is the hardest thing you can do (a lot harder than dentistry, he claims!), but he loves the business because of the food, and mostly because of the people.

1 lb (500 g) beef tenderloin, cut into 1-inch (2.5 cm) cubes

MARINADE

1 Tbsp barbecue sauce
2 tsp soy sauce
1 tsp white vinegar
1 tsp granulated sugar
1 tsp vegetable oil

RICE

1¼ cups water
¾ cup uncooked jasmine rice
pinch of salt
1 tsp ketchup
1 tsp butter
1 tsp granulated sugar

VEGETABLES

2 Tbsp vegetable oil
3 garlic cloves, minced
½ large red pepper, chopped
½ green pepper, chopped
¾ cup sliced onion
¾ cup sliced mushrooms
2 tsp soy sauce
2 tsp sake (or dry sherry)
¾ tsp granulated sugar
pinch of salt

Combine beef and marinade ingredients except vegetable oil in medium non-metallic bowl. Cover and chill for 2 hours if time permits. Heat wok or large frying pan to hot. Add vegetable oil and beef mixture. Stir-fry for 3 to 4 minutes until beef is browned and cooked to your liking. Do not overcook.

To make rice, bring water to a boil in small saucepan. Add rice and salt. Reduce heat to very low. Cook, covered, for 15 minutes; do not remove lid. Let stand for 5 minutes. Fluff with a fork. Add remaining ingredients and stir to combine.

To make vegetables, heat vegetable oil in large frying pan over medium-high. Add garlic, red pepper, green pepper, onion and mushrooms. Add remaining ingredients. Stir-fry for about 3 minutes until vegetables are tender-crisp. Add beef and toss to combine. Serve over rice.

Serves 2

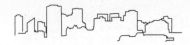

Mom's Cabbage Rolls

Lana Sanderson

My mom poured her heart into everything she did yet made it look effortless and majestic. Her philosophy was to make the kids and her husband happy. She used simple seasonings such as salt, pepper, dill and bay leaves. The aroma was always amazing. I'm convinced it was the way she handled food that brought out the natural sweet and unique flavours. It was mesmerizing to watch the way she held a mixing spoon, the way she moved when she stirred. I always thought Mom knew some kitchen magic.

The family cabbage rolls recipe is the only recipe I took with me when I moved away from home. It's my favorite Russian home-cooked meal that my mom used to make. She had her special trick for how to prep the cabbage—freezing it, instead of boiling or steaming.

The first time I cooked cabbage rolls on my own was for my first serious boyfriend for a Super Bowl party at my place. I called Mom to double-check everything because I really wanted to impress my boyfriend and his friends. He was of Ukrainian descent, and I knew he would be a tough judge. As it turns out, my hands knew exactly what to do and I almost went into a meditation or trance. It was a very peaceful and surreal experience. I pictured my mom in the kitchen with me and I could almost smell her shampoo. The cabbage rolls were a hit, and as it turns out, I was my worst critic. I still am, and I improve my cabbage rolls every time I make them for my husband.

My husband tells me that my cabbage rolls are one of the reasons he married me.

> **1 head cabbage**
> **½ lb (225 g) ground beef**
> **½ lb (225 g) ground pork**
> **1½ cups cooked long-grain white rice**
> **1 medium onion, finely chopped**
> **pinch of salt and freshly ground pepper**
> **1 × 6 oz (170 g) can tomato paste**
> **2 cups water**

Wrap cabbage in plastic wrap and freeze overnight. Remove from freezer and let thaw at room temperature.

Preheat oven to 350° F (175° C). Carefully separate leaves from cabbage. Save only larger leaves for cabbage rolls. Use smaller leaves to cover bottom of ovenproof dish. Remove large centre vein from cabbage leaves to make rolling easier.

Combine beef, pork, rice, onion, salt and pepper in medium bowl.

Place cabbage leaf on board. Place ⅓ to ½ cup of meat mixture in centre of leaf. Fold in sides, then roll up to secure filling. Place, seam-side down, in prepared dish. Repeat with remaining cabbage and filling.

Combine tomato paste and water in small bowl. Pour over cabbage rolls. Bake in preheated oven, covered, for 1 hour until meat is cooked.

Serves 4

Elk Lasagna

Bruce Wells, Homefire Grill

I grew up in Newfoundland, surrounded by fresh, delicious local seafood. I discovered I loved to cook when an old friend of my father's, a chef, convinced me to go to cooking school instead of university. A few years later, I headed for Alberta, where fish may not be plentiful, but jobs were.

I planned to work in Edmonton for two years and then go back to Newfoundland. I didn't realize how much I would love the food industry in this city, and 30 years later, I'm still here.

For 20 years, I owned a Cajun French restaurant, Café Orleans, on Bourbon Street in West Edmonton Mall. Two years ago, it was time for a change. I'm now the chef at the Homefire Grill, which is owned by the Alberta Indian Investment Corporation.

I created this Elk Lasagna as a way to get more wild game on our menu. There may not be a lot of fresh seafood in Alberta, but there is an amazing array of local foods, including wild game meats. I'm a true believer in farmers' markets and I try to source as much local food at the Homefire Grill as possible.

2 Tbsp olive oil, divided
1 lb (500 g) ground elk (or beef)
½ cup finely chopped onion
1 large carrot, peeled and finely chopped
½ cup finely chopped celery
2 cups chopped tomatoes
2 Tbsp tomato paste
1 tsp dried oregano
1 tsp dried basil

½ tsp salt
½ tsp freshly ground pepper
1 cup baby spinach leaves
1 tsp hot sauce
1 cup ricotta cheese
6 lasagna sheets, approximately
2 cups tomato sauce
2 cups grated mozzarella cheese
2 cups grated Cheddar cheese

Preheat oven to 350° F (175° C). Grease shallow medium casserole dish. Heat 1 Tbsp olive oil in large frying pan over medium-high. Cook elk for 5 to 10 minutes, stirring occasionally and breaking up any large lumps, until browned. Remove from pan.

Heat 1 Tbsp olive oil in same pan over medium-high. Add onion, carrot and celery. Cook for about 5 minutes, stirring occasionally, until vegetables are softened. Return elk to same pan.

Add tomatoes, tomato paste, oregano, basil, salt and pepper. Cook for 10 to 12 minutes, stirring occasionally, until tomatoes are broken down and sauce is thickened.

Add spinach and hot sauce. Cook for about 1 minute, stirring, until spinach is wilted. Remove from heat. Stir in ricotta cheese.

Meanwhile, cook pasta in large pot of salted, boiling water for 10 to 12 minutes until tender. Remove from pot.

Spread half of tomato sauce in prepared dish. Top with layer of pasta (cut to fit if necessary). Spoon half of elk mixture evenly over pasta. Sprinkle with one-third of combined mozzarella and Cheddar cheese. Add another layer of pasta, remaining tomato sauce, remaining elk mixture, half of remaining cheese, another layer of pasta and remaining cheese. Cover and bake in preheated oven for 45 minutes. Remove foil. Bake for 20 minutes until top is golden brown. Cover and let stand for 10 minutes before cutting into squares.

Serves 4 to 6

Hardware Grill's Bison Meatloaf with Corn Cheddar Mash

Larry Stewart, Hardware Grill

I grew up on a farm in Ontario. My mom didn't cook elaborate or fancy meals, but it was all rib-sticking good food made from scratch. We had a large vegetable garden and raised our own cattle. My mother canned her own pickles, tomatoes, jams and jellies. This tradition of connecting with food, and with the farmer who made it, is something I carried with me when I opened the Hardware Grill with my wife Melinda 14 years ago. We created this meatloaf recipe for the restaurant when we first opened as a way of updating an old family classic. I knew a few bison farmers, and people were really interested in bison as a local Alberta product. This whole dish, with the ale sauce and mashed potatoes, evokes all the senses of warm comfort food that I remember from my childhood.

To roast corn, cook peeled cobs of corn on a barbecue or hot griddle until charred. Remove kernels by running a knife down the length of each cob. You will need about 3 or 4 cobs (depending on size) for this recipe.

2 Tbsp canola oil

¾ cup finely chopped onion

½ cup finely chopped celery

½ cup finely chopped red pepper

2 tsp salt

1 Tbsp pepper

1½ Tbsp chopped fresh thyme

4 garlic cloves, minced

2 tsp juniper berries, finely chopped

1½ lbs (680 g) ground bison

1½ lbs (680 g) ground veal

3 large eggs

16 bacon slices

McNally's Ale Onion Sauce

2 Tbsp butter

1 cup finely chopped onion

1 × 341 mL bottle Big Rock's McNally's Ale (or a dark beer of your choice)

2 cups demi glaze (rich brown sauce)

pinch of salt and freshly ground pepper

Corn Cheddar Mashed Potatoes

➤ **4 medium new red potatoes, unpeeled and quartered**

4 medium new white potatoes, unpeeled and quartered

⅓ cup melted butter

⅓ cup sour cream

¼ cup cream (or milk), warmed

1½ tsp salt

½ tsp freshly ground pepper

8 oz (225 g) Cheddar cheese, grated

1 cup roasted corn kernels

¼ cup chopped flat leaf (Italian) parsley

Preheat oven to 350° F (175° C). Grease large loaf pan.

Heat olive oil in large frying pan over medium-high. Add onion, celery and red pepper. Cook for 5 minutes until softened. Add salt, pepper, thyme, garlic and juniper berries. Cook for 1 minute until fragrant; drain. Let cool.

Combine onion mixture, bison, veal and eggs in large bowl of electric mixer. Beat until well combined.

Line prepared pan with about 11 bacon slices, slightly overlapping slices. Spoon bison mixture into pan; smooth top. Lay remaining bacon over top. Cover tightly with foil. Bake for 1¼ to 1½ hours until internal temperature reads 155° F (68° C) on meat thermometer when inserted into centre of meatloaf. Let stand in pan for 10 minutes before cutting into slices to serve.

To make onion sauce, melt butter in large frying pan over medium. Cook onion for about 10 minutes, stirring occasionally, until golden brown. Add remaining ingredients. Simmer, uncovered, for about 10 minutes until thickened slightly.

To make mashed potatoes, cook potatoes in salted water in large saucepan over medium until tender; drain. Return to same saucepan. Mash potatoes (skin on) until no large lumps remain (you want potatoes to remain somewhat chunky). Add butter, sour cream, cream, salt and pepper. Fold in remaining ingredients. Serve with meatloaf and sauce.

Serves 8

Bison and Black Bean Chili with Roasted Corn

Albert Tam, Delta Edmonton Centre Suite Hotel

My family immigrated to Edmonton from Hong Kong 32 years ago, when I was still a child. I became interested in food by helping out in the family restaurant my parents opened here.

I like to blend Asian ingredients and western techniques in my recipes. This chili, however, is strictly western. I created it for the annual Chili Cook Off, an event organized by the Edmonton Downtown Business Association every autumn. This chili won the top prize at the Cook Off in 2007 and 2009.

I think the key to success lies in using local bison, which gives it a slightly different flavour and texture. You can also taste the surprising flavours of honey and cinnamon. Most people think of chili as hot and spicy, but you need to balance the spiciness with something sweet.

Of course the Delta cannot win the Chili Cook Off every year, or people will think it's fixed! Last year the Hardware Grill beat us to take home the prize. For the 2011 competition, I may have to tweak the recipe a bit to make sure we still have the best chili in the city.

1 cup frozen, thawed (or fresh) corn kernels

2 Tbsp canola oil

1 onion, finely chopped

8 garlic cloves, minced

1 red pepper, finely chopped

1 green pepper, finely chopped

3 fresh jalapeño peppers, finely chopped

¼ cup chili powder

1 Tbsp cayenne pepper

1 Tbsp paprika

1 Tbsp dried crushed chilies

1½ lbs (680 g) bison sirloin, diced

1½ lbs (680 g) ground bison

2 cups canned black beans, rinsed and drained

1 quart (1 L) apple juice

3 × 14 oz (398 mL) cans crushed tomatoes

3 cinnamon sticks

large pinch of salt and freshly ground pepper

2 Tbsp honey

Preheat oven to 375° F (190° C). Pat corn dry. Place corn in single layer on baking sheet. Roasted in preheated oven for 15 to 20 minutes, stirring occasionally, until lightly browned; set aside.

Heat canola oil in large pot or Dutch oven. Add onion, garlic, red pepper, green pepper and jalapeño peppers. Cook for about 5 minutes, stirring occasionally, until softened.

Add chili powder, cayenne pepper, paprika and chilies. Cook for 1 minute until fragrant. Add all remaining ingredients except honey. Bring to a boil. Reduce to low. Cook, covered, for 2½ hours, stirring occasionally. Remove lid and cook for about 30 minutes, stirring occasionally, until thickened. Stir in honey and serve.

Serves 8

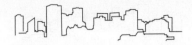

Roast Lamb and Vegetables with Port Sauce

Lovoni Walker, host of Simple, Fresh, Delicious

Being an Aussie, I grew up eating lots of lamb, and today it is still my favourite meat. It is sweet and succulent, and I find it can be quite forgiving for those who aren't too familiar with cooking it. When I head back home to Australia for a holiday, Mum always cooks me a roast lamb dinner. There is no better roast lamb than Mum's, but I think this recipe of mine comes in a close second. If there are any leftovers, slice them up thinly and have them on a sandwich for lunch the next day with some mango chutney—delicious! Lamb can be found fresh and frozen in grocery and specialty food stores.

➤ 3 Tbsp Dijon mustard

2 Tbsp chopped fresh thyme

pinch of salt and freshly ground pepper

4 lbs (2 kg) bone-in lamb leg

4 garlic cloves, quartered

1 Tbsp olive oil

1 lb (500 g) sweet potato (yam), peeled and chopped

3 medium carrots, peeled and chopped

3 medium parsnips, peeled and chopped

3 medium onions, quartered

4 sprigs thyme

4 garlic cloves, bruised

pinch of salt and freshly ground pepper

roasted vegetables to serve (optional)

PORT SAUCE

➤ 2 Tbsp all-purpose flour

2 cups chicken broth (your own or store bought)

½ cup port

½ cup red or black currant jelly

pinch of salt and freshly ground pepper

Preheat oven to 350° F (175° C). Grease wire rack and place in large, shallow roasting pan.

Combine mustard, thyme, salt and pepper in small bowl. Using small, sharp knife, make 16 small incisions over lamb and poke one piece of garlic into each. Rub lamb all over with mustard mixture. Place on prepared wire rack and roast, uncovered, in preheated oven for 1½ to 2 hours until cooked to your liking. Reserve any pan drippings. Cover lamb with foil to keep warm and let stand for 15 minutes before carving.

While lamb is cooking, line large baking sheet with parchment paper. Combine olive oil, sweet potato, carrots, parsnips, onions, thyme, garlic, salt and pepper on prepared baking sheet and arrange in single layer. Roast, uncovered, in oven with lamb for about 1 hour, turning occasionally, until vegetables are browned and tender.

To make port sauce, heat reserved pan drippings in same roasting pan over medium until hot. Add flour and cook for 1 minute, stirring. Stir in remaining ingredients. Bring to a boil and boil gently, uncovered, for 5 to 10 minutes, stirring occasionally, until thickened. Serve sliced lamb with roasted vegetables and sauce.

Serves 6

Bhatia Family Kebabs

Gurvinder Bhatia, Vinomania

My mom has made these kebabs for as long as I can remember. They are a staple and one of our family's true comfort foods. Mom's kebabs are tasty and versatile. You can make them with ground chicken, lamb or beef. You can serve them as hors d'oeuvres. As an entrée, roll them in naan or in a pita pocket with onions, lettuce and tomato, or put them in a hot dog bun with a variety of condiments. Mint chutney is a traditional accompaniment. Mom and Dad grew up in northern India and traditionally the kebabs would have been made in a tandoor (clay oven), but the broiler or grill are acceptable substitutes. They are relatively easy to make, but quality ingredients are key. Strangely, they always taste better when Mom makes them or is "supervising."

As with most handed-down recipes (regardless of the ethnic or cultural background), specific ingredient measurements must be taken with a grain of salt. I've done my best to quantify Mom's "pinch of this," "just the right amount of that," and "I don't know, you just know…" but ultimately the recipe will vary based on your own tastes.

And, of course, no recipe from me would be complete without a wine pairing. As with any style of Indian cuisine, you want to look at wines with a depth of flavour, soft tannins and little or no oak influence. An excellent Indian food wine is the Renwood Sierra Series Zinfandel from the Sierra Foothills in California ($23.99). The ripe fruit and hint of spice are a perfect match to the flavourful kebabs.

- ¾ lb (340 g) ground chicken (or lamb)
- 1 medium yellow onion, finely chopped
- ½ green serrano (or jalapeño) chili pepper, finely chopped
- 1 × 2-inch (5 cm) piece ginger, finely chopped
- 2 Tbsp fine breadcrumbs
- ½ tsp salt
- ⅔ cup chopped cilantro leaves, divided

- vegetable oil
- 6 or 12 metal skewers
- 1 red onion, thinly sliced
- 2 Tbsp lemon juice
- ⅛ tsp chat masala (optional)
- lemon wedges to serve (optional)
- yogurt to serve (optional)
- mint chutney to serve (optional)

Place greased piece of aluminum foil on baking sheet.

Combine chicken, yellow onion, chili pepper, ginger, breadcrumbs, salt and two-thirds of cilantro in medium bowl; mix well.

Divide mixture into 6 or 12. Rub a little vegetable oil on your hands and shape some of the mixture around skewer to make long kebab shape, ensuring even thickness. Repeat with remaining chicken mixture. Place kebabs on prepared baking sheet and broil for 12 to 20 minutes (depending on size of kebabs), turning occasionally, until cooked.

Meanwhile, combine red onion and lemon juice in small bowl.

Place kebabs on serving platter. Sprinkle with chat masala, if desired, remaining cilantro and red onion mixture. Serve with yogurt and/or mint chutney and lemon wedges if desired.

Makes 6 large or 12 small kebabs

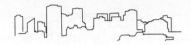

Maple Chicken

George Sellmer

I've always liked to experiment with food. I grew up in a small town near Toronto. In the late 1960s, I met some people who were vegetarian, back to the land and organically minded, and found myself attracted to that whole philosophy. It was part of a spiritual awakening. We went on to start what was I believe was the first natural foods restaurant in Toronto.

These days I'm eating more meat and much fewer carbs, almost the opposite of when I first became aware of nutrition four decades ago. Go figure. I tend to be very simple in my tastes and will stick with a basic menu, with variations, for weeks. I can't remember when or how I came up with this recipe, just throwing things into the pan and experimenting, I guess. I still make this because the kids really like it, and they are fussy.

> **8 boneless, skinless chicken thighs,
>   cut into 1-inch (2.5 cm) cubes**
> **⅓ cup teriyaki sauce (such as Kikkoman's)**
> **2 Tbsp maple syrup**
> **1 tsp garlic powder**
> **steamed fragrant rice to serve (optional)**

Combine chicken, teriyaki sauce, maple syrup and garlic powder in medium bowl. Cover and place in refrigerator for 5 minutes.

Heat large frying pan or wok over medium-high. Add chicken and marinade. Cook for 7 to 8 minutes, stirring occasionally, until chicken is cooked and glazed. Serve with rice if desired.

Serves 4

Black Pepper Chicken
Munira Shariff

My husband never used to eat chicken. One day my friend and neighbour sent me some of this chicken and guaranteed that my husband would eat it and like it, too. And guess what? He got hooked on this one. I asked my friend for the recipe but she wouldn't tell me what it was, so I made up my own recipe, relying entirely on my taste buds. Now I cook it at least twice a month, which is a lot considering my husband never liked chicken before.

➤ ¼ **cup tomato paste**
½ **bunch cilantro, chopped**
pinch of salt
1 **Tbsp freshly ground black pepper**
2 **Tbsp olive oil**
8 **boneless, skinless chicken thighs, quartered**
½ **cup water**
steamed rice to serve (optional)

Place tomato paste, cilantro, salt and pepper in food processor. Process until finely chopped and mixture has formed paste.

Heat olive oil in large frying pan over medium-high. Cook chicken for 5 to 10 minutes until browned. Add cilantro mixture. Reduce heat to medium-low. Cook, covered, for about 15 minutes, stirring occasionally and adding a little water if necessary, until chicken is cooked. Serve with rice if desired.

Serves 4

Roast Turkey with Slow Cooker Stuffing and Cranberry Orange Relish

This recipe is courtesy of Fill-Up, the Community Ambassador for Edmonton's Food Bank. The grocery bag–shaped mascot and ambassador, with the bushy eyebrows and ready grin, shares a birthday with the Food Bank: January 1981. Fill-Up enjoys meeting people and giving hugs. His social calendar is very busy but he would still love to meet you; find out more at edmontonsfoodbank.com. Fill-Up's favorite pastime is cooking.

SLOW COOKER STUFFING

- 3 cups coarse breadcrumbs
- 1 lb (500 g) bulk sausage, browned and drained
- ¼ cup butter
- 1 cup finely chopped onion
- 1 cup finely chopped celery
- 1 finely chopped fennel bulb (optional)
- 1 × 10 oz (284 mL) can mushrooms, un-drained
- ¼ cup chopped fresh parsley
- 2 tsp poultry seasoning
- ½ tsp salt
- pinch of freshly ground pepper
- 2 large eggs, lightly beaten
- 1 quart (1 L) chicken broth
- 2 medium apples, peeled, cored and chopped
- 1 cup whole cranberries (fresh, or frozen and thawed)

CRANBERRY ORANGE RELISH

- ½ cup water
- ½ cup orange juice
- 1 cup granulated sugar
- ½ cup chopped dried apricots
- 1 lb (500 g) whole cranberries (fresh, or frozen and thawed)
- 2 Tbsp finely grated orange zest
- 2 Tbsp finely grated ginger

TURKEY

- 1 turkey
- 1 medium onion, chopped
- 2 medium carrots, peeled and chopped
- 4 celery stalks, chopped
- ¼ cup butter, softened
- ½ tsp dried sage
- ½ tsp dried rosemary
- ½ tsp salt
- ½ tsp freshly ground pepper
- ¼ cup all-purpose flour
- 1 quart (1 L) chicken broth
- pinch of salt and freshly ground pepper

To make stuffing, combine breadcrumbs and sausage in large bowl; set aside. Melt butter in large frying pan over medium-high. Add onion, celery and fennel if desired. Cook for about 5 minutes, stirring occasionally, until softened. Add to breadcrumb mixture. Add remaining ingredients and stir until well combined. Place in large slow cooker. Cook for 1 hour on high. Reduce heat to low and cook for 3 hours.

To make cranberry orange relish, combine water, orange juice and sugar in medium saucepan. Stir over medium until sugar is dissolved. Add remaining ingredients and bring to boil over high. Cook, uncovered, for about 10 minutes, stirring occasionally, until skins of cranberries begin to pop. Seal in sterilized jars. Makes about 3 cups.

To make turkey, preheat oven to 425° F (220° C). Remove neck and giblets from turkey. Rinse turkey inside and out with cold running water. Pat dry with paper towel. Put onion, carrots and celery in large roasting pan. Combine butter, sage, rosemary, salt and pepper in small bowl. Place turkey on vegetables in roasting pan. Rub butter mixture all over turkey, placing some between skin and breast meat. Cover loosely with foil.

Cook turkey for 30 minutes. Reduce oven temperature to 325° F (160° C). Baste turkey every hour during cooking. Cooking times: 10 lbs (4.5 kg), 2¾–3 hours; 14 lbs (6.3 kg), 3–3¼ hours; 18 lbs (8.2 kg), 4–4½ hours; 24 lbs (10.8 kg), 4½–5 hours. Remove foil for last 30 minutes. Cook until juices run clear when sharp knife is inserted into thigh area or when internal temperature reaches 170° F (76° C). Remove turkey to cutting board. Cover with foil and let rest for 15 minutes before carving. Reserve pan juices and vegetables in pan.

Heat roasting pan over medium. Add flour. Cook for 1 minute, stirring. Gradually stir in broth. Cook for about 10 minutes, stirring occasionally, until thickened; strain. Add salt and pepper to taste. Serve turkey with stuffing, relish and gravy.

Serves 10 to 12

Tandoori Chicken on Your Home Grill

Shiraz Kanji

In a way, the story of this tandoori chicken recipe traces the story of how my family came to live in Canada over 30 years ago.

I grew up in Tanzania and studied at the University of Nairobi in the early 1970s. It was there that I had my first taste of tandoori chicken, or chicken tikka as it was called there. A few years after I finished my studies, my family left Tanzania for Canada. People of Indian descent were having an increasingly difficult time in East Africa, and Canada was one of the more desirable countries to immigrate to. I ended up in Edmonton and, despite the snowy climate, I was surprised by how much it reminded me of Nairobi. I immediately felt at home.

When I left Tanzania, I never thought I would eat tandoori chicken or naan in Canada, never mind create a recipe of my own and share it with others. But now friends and family here are always asking me for the recipe. This dish is based on that first tandoori chicken I tried in Nairobi. How many of us in Canada actually have a tandoor (clay oven) at home? I certainly don't. So I created the recipe with a grill in mind. The basics for any tandoori chicken recipe are pretty common, but I added sour cream and saffron to make it a little fancier and tastier. Later, I also started adding cornstarch and substituted commercial tandoori paste in place of spices once it became available. The key is to put the saffron in warm water first so it mixes well. As most cooks know, the proportions in a recipe are often an approximate measure. Feel free to adjust these ingredients to your palate. And then be prepared for a tasty adventure.

> 12 boneless, skinless chicken thighs, halved

MARINADE

> ⅓ cup plain yogurt
> ¼ cup sour cream
> 2 Tbsp tandoori paste
> 2 garlic cloves, minced
> 1 tsp finely grated ginger
> 2 Tbsp lemon juice
> 2 tsp cornstarch
> ½ tsp salt
> 2 Tbsp canola oil
> ½ tsp ground cumin
> ½ tsp ground coriander
> 1 tsp sambal oelek (chili paste)
> 10 saffron threads (optional)

To make marinade, combine all ingredients in medium non-metallic bowl.

Add chicken and stir to coat. Cover and refrigerate for 8 hours or overnight if time permits.

Preheat greased grill to medium. Cook chicken for 5 to 8 minutes per side until cooked.

Serves 6

Honey Curry Chicken

Susan Kellock, Skinny Legs and Cowgirls

Making this dish makes me think of my mother, who is no longer with us. She was a literary agent and did a lot of entertaining when I was growing up. I remember helping her cook the fancy food for her dinner parties. She used to get mad at me because her hollandaise would split and mine wouldn't! I think the idea to become a chef was first planted while cooking at my mother's side.

This is a dish my mother used to make for me and my siblings when we were growing up. It's a very simple dish, but it will turn any child who doesn't like curry into a curry-lover. For that reason I call it a converting dish! As a mother myself, I made it frequently for my kids and it was a hit at parties. I used to get accosted by all the other parents for the recipe.

> **1 Tbsp canola oil**
> **6 chicken drumsticks**
> **6 chicken thighs**
> **½ cup honey**
> **¼ cup butter**
> **1 Tbsp prepared (or Dijon) mustard**
> **1 Tbsp curry powder (hot or mild)**
> **steamed brown basmati rice to serve**
> **steamed broccoli to serve**

Preheat oven to 350° F (175° C). Grease large casserole dish.

Heat canola oil in large frying pan on medium-high. Cook chicken in batches for about 5 minutes until browned all over. Remove from pan to prepared dish.

Add remaining ingredients to same frying pan. Stir over medium until butter is melted. Pour over chicken. Cover with foil. Bake for 30 minutes. Remove foil and turn chicken. Bake for 30 minutes more until tender and cooked through. Serve with rice and broccoli if desired.

Serves 6

Kabuli Pulao

Ziaudeen Adil, NorQuest College student

I'm from Afghanistan but I've been living in Edmonton for three years. I came because I was leaving the bad situation in Afghanistan. My uncle sponsored me to come and make a better life in a peaceful country. Now I'm so happy and proud to be in Canada. I see a bright future for my family here.

This recipe is a traditional and very famous food in Afghanistan, and is often made for celebrations like weddings and birthdays. When I first arrived in Canada, we went to my uncle's house—myself, my mom, my dad, my sister, my brother and my children. We all sat down to eat our first meal in Canada together, and this is what we ate. We celebrated our fresh start but remembered where we came from at the same time.

2¼ cups uncooked long-grain white rice

2 Tbsp vegetable oil

2 lbs (1 kg) boneless, skinless chicken breasts, chopped

3 medium onions, finely chopped

4 large carrots, peeled and finely chopped

8 garlic cloves, minced

2 tsp granulated sugar

pinch of salt and freshly ground pepper

2½ cups dark raisins

3 large tomatoes, cored and chopped

1 quart (1 L) chicken broth (or water)

| **Place** rice in large bowl. Cover with water. Let stand for 8 hours or overnight; drain.

Heat vegetable oil in large frying pan over medium-high. Cook chicken in 4 or more batches until browned. Remove to pot; set aside.

Add onions and carrots to same pan, adding a little extra oil if needed. Cook for about 10 minutes, stirring occasionally, until softened. Add garlic and cook for 1 to 2 minutes until fragrant. Stir in sugar, salt and pepper. Add to pot with chicken.

Stir in rice and remaining ingredients. Bring to a boil. Reduce heat to low. Cook, covered, for 25 to 30 minutes until rice is tender and chicken is cooked.

Serves 8 to 10

Dakabaw

Hse Nay Paw, NorQuest College student

Dakabaw is pronounced "Ta Ka Paw." There are about 300 Karen refugees living in Edmonton. Thanks to Dr. Alice Khin for helping refine this submission.

This is a traditional Karen food. The Karen people are a minority group in Burma, also known as Myanmar. In times gone by, when Karen people had few cooking tools or condiments, this is how we prepared our food. We would dry the chicken in the sun so we could boil it with fresh vegetables and rice to make a delicious stew.

Though I cannot go back to Burma, this meal reminds me of home. We eat this when celebrating Karen New Year or Christmas Day. And it is served for special days when guests come to our home or when there is a wedding. This dish was also made to honour the visit of a grandparent. My grandmother taught me how to make Dakabaw when I was 20, and I will carry on the tradition here in Edmonton.

1 × 3 lb (1.4 kg) whole chicken, rinsed
   and dried
3 quarts (3 L) water
pinch of salt
1 Tbsp vegetable oil
1 large onion, chopped

4 garlic cloves, minced
1 Tbsp finely grated fresh ginger
1 cup uncooked long-grain rice, rinsed
2 Tbsp dry mustard
1 tsp dried bamboo shoot
   (soaked overnight and drained)

In water in pot, cook chicken over medium for about 1½ hours until tender. Remove chicken from cooking liquid; reserve liquid. Add salt to liquid. Remove meat from bones; discard skin and bones. Chop meat into small pieces; set aside.

Heat vegetable oil in pot. Add onion, garlic and ginger. Cook for about 5 minutes, stirring occasionally, until tender.

Add rice and stir to coat. Add reserved chicken liquid, mustard and bamboo shoot. Cook, uncovered, for 10 minutes. Stir in reserved chicken meat. Cook for about 5 minutes until chicken is hot and rice is tender.

Serves 4

Chicken Breasts with Green Peas

Olga Anastase, NorQuest College student

My mother cooked this for me when I was a child. I can distinctly remember the aroma of this dish and it always reminds me of my mother. Now this is my family's favourite food, and that is great because it's easy to make. When my son was 3 years old he couldn't speak very well, but if he wanted to eat the chicken with green peas he used to say, "Mama, can you cook small balls for me?" It has become my family's comfort food.

2 Tbsp vegetable oil
1 lb (500 g) boneless, skinless chicken breasts, chopped
1 medium onion, chopped
1 garlic clove, minced
1 cup chicken broth (or water)
1 cup tomato sauce
1 tsp salt
½ tsp freshly ground pepper
2 cups frozen peas

Heat vegetable oil in large, deep frying pan over medium-high. Cook chicken in 2 or 3 batches until browned; set aside.

Add onion and garlic to same frying pan. Cook for about 5 minutes, stirring occasionally, until softened. Return chicken to pan. Reduce heat to medium.

Add broth, tomato sauce, salt and pepper. Cook, uncovered, for about 10 minutes, stirring occasionally, until chicken is cooked and sauce is thickened.

Add peas and cook, covered, for about 5 minutes until peas are cooked.

Serves 4

Organic Chicken Dinner

Adele and Brian Draper

I'm inspired by my grandparents' approach to eating and living. My grandfather, Dr. Severin Sabourin, was the first mayor and family practitioner from Bonnyville, Alberta, in the early 1930s. He would often go by horse and buggy and then by car to provide emergency services such as delivering babies. My grandmother, along with her 14 children, would receive bushels of potatoes, grain and other goods as payment. All of this was, of course, organic, home-grown and free of pesticides. They ate simply and gloriously! When we were raising our family, we were always careful to cook and grow our own ingredients. I made my own baby food and used cloth diapers, not because it was current but because it was cost-effective. I took great pride in making food from scratch as my mother and her mother before her did.

My husband and I recently joined the Slow Food movement out of Italy that stresses organic and local food. Now that we are completely into organic as a way of health, we understand that most people need to take "baby steps" if the community at large is to achieve a more sustainable way of eating and living. As a high school art teacher, I urge my students to eschew the grease of fast food and eat in more healthy ways. As they work away on their art projects, I share horror stories of hormones, antibiotics and bad animal treatment in the industry. Today, one of my students brought fresh veggies as a snack—yes, baby steps.

And the learning at home? Recently my daughter (in her second year of university) declared she feels more energetic and less stressed since the family switched to an organic and more healthy style of cooking. Imagine that!

> **5 lbs (2.5 kg) chicken, preferably organic**
> **2 tsp olive oil**
> **1 tsp sea salt**
> **1 tsp powdered garlic**
> **½ tsp dried rosemary**
> **½ tsp freshly ground pepper**
> **½ cup water**
> **1 tsp granulated sugar**

Parmesan Crostini

8 to 12 small bread slices (or 4 to 6 regular size)
butter for spreading
1 cup finely grated fresh Parmesan cheese

Preheat oven to 375° F (190° C). Place chicken in ovenproof dish. Drizzle with olive oil. Sprinkle with salt inside and out. Sprinkle with garlic, rosemary and pepper. Pour water into dish and add sugar. Bake in preheated oven, covered, for 45 minutes. Remove cover. Bake, uncovered, for about 1 hour until juices run clear when chicken is pieced in leg and thigh area. Cover and let stand for 15 minutes before carving. Reserve drippings.

To make crostini, toast bread lightly. Spread each slice with a little butter. Top with Parmesan cheese. Bake on baking sheet in preheated oven for 5 to 7 minutes until golden. Serve with chicken and some chicken pan drippings, with a tossed garden salad drizzled with balsamic dressing on the side.

Serves 6 to 8

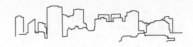

Paw Pia Thawt
(Thai Spring Rolls)

Eric Wah, The King and I Restaurant

I grew up in Hong Kong, where I learned how to cook from my mother. After graduating from university in Canada, I started to work in restaurants. On a family trip to Bangkok in 1986, I fell in love with Thai food. Since there were no Thai restaurants in Alberta, I decided to open one. My first restaurant was in Calgary, and in 1991 I opened The King and I, the first Thai restaurant in Edmonton.

I love Thai food because of all the different fragrances, tastes and textures. It has a lot of influences from Chinese and Indian cooking, but adds local flavours like chili peppers and fresh herbs. Spring rolls, for example, originated in China, but each Asian country has put its own spin on them. Every Thai restaurant in Edmonton adds a special touch to make their rolls stand out from all the others. At The King and I, we use taro root as our special ingredient. It adds a fragrant nutty flavour to the ground pork, and the soft texture contrasts with the chewy silver noodles and crispy outer shell.

➤ **1 egg**
1 Tbsp all-purpose flour
2 oz (55 g) bean thread noodles
1 tsp canola oil
¼ cup grated taro root
¼ cup grated carrot
½ lb (225 g) ground pork
2 Tbsp fish sauce
1 Tbsp grated palm sugar (or brown sugar)
½ tsp freshly ground pepper
1 package 8-inch (20 cm) spring roll wrappers
canola oil for deep-frying

Chili Lime Dipping Sauce

➤ ½ cup sugar

¼ cup water

¼ cup fish sauce

2 Tbsp lime juice

1½ tsp sambal oelek (chili paste)

1 garlic clove, minced

1 Tbsp chopped peanuts

Combine egg and flour in small bowl; set aside. Place noodles in heatproof dish. Cover with boiling water. Let stand for 5 minutes; drain. Cut noodles into shorter lengths; set aside.

Heat canola oil in small frying pan over medium-high. Add taro root and carrot and cook for about 5 minutes until softened; set aside.

Combine noodles, taro root mixture, pork, fish sauce, sugar and pepper in medium bowl. Place a spring roll wrapper on work surface. Place about 2 Tbsp of mixture into centre of wrapper. Brush edge of wrapper with egg mixture. Fold up corner of wrapper closest to you over pork mixture. Fold in sides. Roll up to enclose filling. Repeat with remaining wrappers, pork mixture and egg mixture.

Deep-fry in batches in hot oil for about 3 minutes until golden brown. Drain on paper towel.

To make dipping sauce, stir sugar, water and fish sauce in small saucepan over medium until sugar dissolves. Remove from heat. Add lime juice, sambal oelek and garlic. Pour into serving bowl. Sprinkle with peanuts. Serve spring rolls with dipping sauce.

Makes about 22

Potato Crust Quiche

Esther Morgan, volunteer for Edmonton's Food Bank

I was diagnosed with celiac disease 13 years ago, and this was the first recipe that someone found for me as I began to change what I ate. My daughter's mother-in-law loved to cook and she owned dozens of cookbooks. When she heard about my diagnosis, she remembered seeing a recipe for celiacs and looked it up. It was originally made with grated potatoes, but being the lazy cook that I am, I changed it to hash browns.

> **3 cups frozen hash browns, thawed**
> **3 Tbsp vegetable oil**
> **1 large onion, finely chopped**
> **1 cup chopped ham (or cooked and chopped chicken, sausage, salmon, tuna or shrimp)**
> **1 cup grated Cheddar cheese**
> **3 large eggs**
> **½ cup milk (2% MF)**
> **pinch of salt and freshly ground pepper**

Preheat oven to 425° F (220° C). Grease quiche pan or deep-dish pie plate.

Combine hash browns and vegetable oil in medium bowl. Press onto base and up sides of prepared dish, pressing hash browns to make them stick. Bake in preheated oven, uncovered, for 15 minutes.

Reduce oven temperature to 350° F (175° C). Scatter onion, ham and cheese over hash brown crust.

Whisk eggs, milk, salt and pepper in medium bowl. Pour over filling. Bake for 30 minutes. Reduce oven temperature to 325° F (160° C). Cook for about 10 minutes until knife inserted into centre comes out clean. Cut into wedges to serve.

Serves 4 to 6

Brazilian Beans
Cássia Migliorança

This is a very typical food from Brazil. Most of the Brazilians who come to Canada (especially to Edmonton), including myself, miss not only barbecue, but also Brazilian Beans. I lived in the south of Brazil until I was 18 and then moved to the southeast, where I learned to make Brazilian Beans from a boyfriend's mother.

Since moving to Canada, I've made this dish more often here than in my home country. One of my colleagues from the university tried it and said that it was the best bean recipe she had ever tasted. Sometimes I really miss home flavours, so cooking is one way to overcome that feeling.

7 oz (200 g) pepperoni, thinly sliced

7 oz (200 g) bacon slices, chopped

1 large onion, chopped

4 garlic cloves, minced

1 side of pork ribs, cut into individual ribs

2 cups water

3 × 14 oz (398 mL) cans black beans, rinsed and drained

1 bay leaf

pinch of salt and freshly ground pepper

steamed rice for serving (optional)

Heat large frying pan over medium-high. Add pepperoni and bacon. Cook for about 5 minutes, stirring occasionally, until browned. Remove to paper towel. Drain fat from pan.

Return pepperoni and bacon to same pan. Add onion. Cook for about 5 minutes, stirring occasionally, until onion is softened. Add garlic and cook for about 1 minute until fragrant.

Remove onion mixture from pan. Add ribs to same pan. Cook for about 10 minutes, turning occasionally, until browned. Place ribs, pepperoni mixture, water, beans, bay leaf, salt and pepper in pot. Add remaining ingredients and stir. Cook, covered, over medium for about 20 minutes, stirring occasionally, until mixture is thickened.

Remove bay leaf. Serve with rice if desired.

Serves 4

Jack Daniels Crock Pot Ribs

Ron Leckelt

I have been preparing barbecue ribs for years, but the recipes I used were never the same and the results never seemed quite right. The taste was okay, but I wanted outstanding. I had always boiled my ribs first to remove the excess fat, usually because I barbecued them and didn't want any flare-ups from the grease. Then a few years ago I bought a crock pot and started transforming a lot of my recipes. I haven't boiled my ribs since. It seemed silly to throw a lot of the rib flavour down the drain with the water. It didn't take long before my rib recipe evolved. A group of my friends started getting together for various house parties—birthdays, Grey Cup day, etc.—and everyone was asked to bring a dish. I sprung my JD ribs on them to a great response. Since then I've mixed it up and sometimes used dark rum, and some of my friends preferred the ribs that way. Either way, these ribs are a big hit!

3–4 lbs (1.4–1.8 kg) racks baby back pork ribs
1 bottle barbecue sauce
  (such as Bull's Eye Original)
1 cup Jack Daniels (or dark rum)
1 large onion, finely chopped
1 large green pepper, finely chopped
1 large red pepper, finely chopped
½ cup packed brown sugar

¼ cup cider vinegar
½ cup tomato paste
2 Tbsp Worcestershire sauce
2 Tbsp garlic powder
1 Tbsp Dijon mustard
pinch of freshly ground pepper

Cut each slab of ribs into individual ribs. Place in single layer on greased baking sheet (it may be necessary to do this in more than one batch). Broil for about 15 minutes, turning occasionally, until golden brown. Place ribs into large slow cooker.

Combine remaining ingredients in medium saucepan. Stir over medium until sugar is dissolved. Pour over ribs. Cook on low for 8 to 10 hours until meat is falling off bones.

Serves 6 to 8

Ida's Ribs

Tom Thurston

When I was growing up in Red Deer, it became a family tradition that when my brother, sisters and many relatives came together, we could count on my mom to make a giant batch of homemade ribs. We called them Ida's Ribs. She served them with homemade coleslaw and baked potatoes that were perfect for sopping up the extra yummy sauce. These ribs are so good that my cousin Richard would drive in from Rocky Mountain House so that he wouldn't miss out.

> **4 racks baby back ribs**
> **2 Tbsp garlic powder**
> **1½ cups ketchup**
> **¼ cup malt vinegar**
> **¼ cup packed brown sugar**
> **2 tsp dry mustard**
> **2 tsp Worcestershire sauce**
> **4 tsp grated lemon zest**
> **¼ cup lemon juice**
> **1 large onion, finely chopped**

Preheat oven to 325° F (160° C). Grease large roasting pan.

Cut each rack of ribs into two-rib sections. Place in prepared pan. Sprinkle both sides with garlic powder. Bake, uncovered, in preheated oven for about 40 minutes, turning occasionally, until browned; drain fat from pan.

Combine remaining ingredients in small bowl. Drizzle over ribs, turning to coat. Bake, uncovered, for about 40 minutes until tender and sticky.

Serves 6

Slow-Cooked Ribs

Mark Harvey, CBC Edmonton

First I have a confession: to paraphrase Nixon, "I am not a cook!" I am either a spoiled layabout, or a wizard with steak and potatoes. But last summer's great deals on pork prompted me to go slightly outside my "rare, turn it once" comfort zone. So here is my recipe for slow-cooked ribs on a gas grill.

There's nothing worse than burnt, crunchy, charcoaled ribs. And the reason is always cooking them too fast. I know, I've done it, and eaten the results. If you only have a gas grill (like I do), make sure it will turn down low enough. Over 300° F (150° C), and you're risking wasting good ribs. Test your grill first: after preheating, see if your grill will then maintain 200° F (95° C).

Prepare a rub. This one's good: it's called a Carolina rub. The result doesn't give you quite the southern BBQ taste famous in the Carolinas (we're working with gas here), but I have some good memories of the Oilers' Cup run in 2006 and following them to Raleigh. And I just like the taste.

You will need a large shallow disposable baking ban or deep baking sheet; a disposable tin roasting pan works well for this. Make sure it will fit between your burners and the grill.

Start early in the day—let ribs marinate for 4 hours before cooking—and stay off the beer until dinnertime because this needs time. You will have at least 3 hours to make your salads and other dishes.

> **2 Tbsp salt**
> **2 Tbsp granulated sugar**
> **2 Tbsp brown sugar**
> **2 Tbsp ground cumin**
> **2 Tbsp chili powder**
> **2 Tbsp freshly ground pepper**
> **1 Tbsp cayenne pepper**
> **¼ cup paprika**
> **2–4 racks ribs**
> **barbecue sauce (optional)**

Combine salt, both sugars, cumin, chili powder, pepper, cayenne pepper and paprika in small bowl. Rub liberally over both sides of ribs (save any leftover rub mixture in small container). Place ribs on baking sheet in single layer. Refrigerate for up to 4 hours if time permits.

Place heat-resistant container half-filled with water under barbecue grill. Make sure it fits between burners and grill.

Preheat barbecue to high, then reduce temperate to low. Using indirect heating method, cook ribs over unlit side at about 200° F to 250° F (95° C to 120° C) for about 2½ to 3 hours until ribs are tender, replenishing water when necessary. Cooking time will vary depending on how hot your barbecue gets. Brush with your favourite barbecue sauce if desired.

Serves 4 to 6

Crabmeat Wraps

Barbara Gregory

My nonna and nonno emigrated from Italy shortly after World War I and settled in Lethbridge. Nonna created simple, tasty meals for her visiting clan, usually me with my parents and four brothers. We would gather downstairs in the summer kitchen and drink homemade wine with the meal.

My mother also cooked simply. She used few sauces and rarely bought anything canned. She had a collection of cookbooks, including *The Woman's Favourite Cook Book* from 1949, and she can look at a recipe and tell you in a second if it's worth buying the ingredients.

As for me, I like to experiment, try a little of this and that. While driving home from work I usually plan our supper meal in my head. This recipe came from one of those commutes. I knew I had a package of peppers in the fridge and calories to count, and half an hour later our new family favourite was born. The preparation time is under 30 minutes if you can slice quickly. Any leftovers make a great lunch item for work.

1 Tbsp olive oil
1 medium onion, thinly sliced
1 small red pepper, thinly sliced
1 small yellow pepper, thinly sliced
1 small orange pepper, thinly sliced
8 medium white mushrooms, thinly sliced
pinch of salt and freshly ground pepper

1 package imitation crabmeat
   (or sliced cooked chicken or beef)
½ cup light cream cheese, divided
4 large sun-dried tomato tortillas
   (or your choice)
2 cups baby spinach leaves

Heat olive oil in large frying pan over medium-high. Add onion, peppers, mushrooms, salt and pepper. Cook for 5 to 10 minutes, stirring occasionally, until softened. Add crabmeat and stir until warm.

Spread about 2 Tbsp cream cheese onto each tortilla. Place some spinach leaves down centre of each tortilla. Add onion mixture on top of spinach. Roll up to secure filling.

Makes 4

Polvo
(Portuguese Octopus Stew)
Pedro Tavares

This recipe is my variant of the traditional Polvo and has been my favourite meal for as long as I can remember. One of the changes that I made to the more common recipe is that I added white wine instead of red wine (try the red sometime to see if you agree). Growing up in such a multicultural nation as Canada, I was exposed to various types of food, hence the wonderful addition of the Vietnamese Bo Kho cubes.

I have introduced this delicious stew to several people from many different cultures across Canada. Everyone has enjoyed it thoroughly (even people who would never have envisioned themselves eating octopus).

1½ lbs (680 g) octopus
1 medium onion, chopped
4 garlic cloves, minced
1 bunch parsley, trimmed
2 tsp ground paprika
1 Tbsp sambal oelek (chili paste)
1 tsp ground cumin
2 bay leaves
3 Tbsp olive oil
1 cup dry white wine

2 cups water
pinch of salt and freshly ground pepper
2 medium potatoes, peeled and cubed
2 medium carrots, peeled and cubed
2 cubes Bo Kho Vietnamese soup base
   (or 2 chicken stock cubes)
¼ tsp ground cinnamon (optional)
crusty bread to serve (optional)
steamed rice to serve (optional)

Combine octopus, onion, garlic, parsley, paprika, sambal oelek, cumin, bay leaves, olive oil, wine, water, salt and pepper in large pot. Bring to a boil, then reduce heat to medium-low. Cook, covered, for 1½ hours.

Add potatoes, carrots and cubes. Cook, covered, for about 30 minutes until vegetables are cooked and octopus is tender. Remove bay leaves.

Stir in cinnamon if desired. Serve with bread or steamed rice on the side if desired.

Serves 6

Tomato Coriander Ratatouille with Halibut

Jane Zaiane

In our family, food and family time always go hand in hand. No matter how busy we get, breakfast and dinner are family affairs. And though it can be a challenge at times, almost everything is made from scratch. Take-out is not an option. I think that is a bit of a family tradition. My cooking inspiration is my grandfather; he was a confectioner who made everything from scratch.

Now, we only have one cookbook in the house and it's filled with handwritten recipes. Most of them were created here in our kitchen, like this recipe. When you throw caution to the wind and experiment with what you have on hand, you can end up with some surprising successes. For example, it may seem a little unusual to throw mint into a ratatouille like this, but it's absolutely delicious. This recipe is now one of our family favourites. The children love fried fish and hot pepper, and the parents love unusual ratatouille dishes. It allows me to satisfy our family's diverse tastes—and we can all look forward to sitting down at the end of the day to enjoy it together.

RATATOUILLE

- 1 Tbsp olive oil
- 1 medium onion, chopped
- 2 garlic cloves, minced
- 4 large ripe tomatoes, chopped
- 1 tsp tomato paste
- 1 tsp harissa paste (or ½ tsp chili powder)
- 2 cups chopped curly kale
- ½ cup fresh cilantro leaves, chopped
- ½ cup fresh mint leaves, chopped

HALIBUT

- 1 Tbsp olive oil
- 1 tsp ground cumin
- ½ tsp cayenne pepper
- ½ tsp ground coriander
- pinch of salt and freshly ground pepper
- 1 × 10 oz (280 g) halibut fillet, cut into bite-sized pieces

Heat olive oil in large frying pan over medium-high. Add onion and garlic and cook for about 5 minutes until softened.

Stir in tomatoes, tomato paste and harissa paste. Reduce heat to medium. Cook, covered, for about 10 minutes, stirring occasionally, until tomatoes are broken down and sauce is thickened.

Add kale and stir to combine. Cook, covered, for 5 to 10 minutes until kale is tender. Stir in remaining ingredients.

Meanwhile, combine olive oil, cumin, cayenne pepper, coriander, salt, pepper and halibut in medium bowl. Heat large frying pan over medium. Cook halibut until flesh flakes easily when tested with a fork. Spoon halibut into ratatouille mixture. Stir gently to combine.

Serves 4

Halibut Cheeks, Potato Rosti and Succotash

David Omar, Zinc Restaurant

At our restaurant in the new art gallery, we try to take your usual comfort foods and put a little twist on them. When we first opened, we toured the gallery with the curators to find inspiration in the art. I was also fortunate to be able to sit down with artist George Miller when he had an exhibit in the gallery and come up with menu items that would reflect his art.

This dish is a bit of a nod to growing up in New Brunswick. It's where I developed my love of food. I grew up on a farm where everything was freshly sourced and my mom would always cook from scratch. There was a lake right across the street where we could catch fresh fish. So this halibut dish is like an upscale fish and chips, with an artistic twist, of course.

POTATO ROSTI

1 lb (500 g) Yukon Gold potatoes, peeled
¼ cup butter, melted
2 Tbsp fresh chopped rosemary
1 tsp salt
1 tsp freshly ground pepper
duck fat (or olive oil or butter) for frying

EDAMAME AND CORN SUCCOTASH

4 Tbsp butter
1½ cups fresh, cooked corn kernels
   (or frozen, thawed)
1½ cups shelled, cooked edamame
¼ cup cream
1 tsp salt
¼ tsp freshly ground pepper
finely chopped red pepper to serve (optional)
finely chopped parsley to serve (optional)

HALIBUT CHEEKS

> **1 lb (500 g) halibut (or other fish) cheeks (or fillets)**
> **pinch of salt and freshly ground pepper**
> **2 Tbsp butter**

| Preheat oven to 400° F (205° C). Lightly grease baking sheet.

Coarsely grate potatoes. Place in colander or wrap in tea towel and press or squeeze to remove excess liquid. Combine potatoes, butter, rosemary, salt and pepper in medium bowl.

Heat 1–2 Tbsp of fat in large frying pan (preferably cast-iron) over medium-high. Drop ¼ cup of potato mixture into pan, spreading mixture out so it cooks evenly. Reduce heat to medium. Cook for about 3 to 5 minutes per side until golden. Remove to prepared baking sheet in single layer. Repeat with remaining potato mixture, adding more fat as needed and ensuring fat is hot before adding potato. Bake potatoes on baking sheet in preheated oven for about 10 minutes until hot and crisp.

To make succotash, melt butter in large frying pan over medium. Add corn, edamame and cream. Cook for 5 to 10 minutes, stirring occasionally, until hot. Add salt and pepper. Garnish with red pepper or parsley if desired.

To make halibut cheeks, pat halibut dry. Sprinkle with salt and pepper. Melt butter in large frying pan over medium-high. Cook halibut in 2 batches for about 5 minutes until just cooked. Serve with potato rosti and succotash.

Serves 4

Lebanese-Style Sea Bass with Olives, Tomatoes and Garlic

Joe Rustom, Parkallen Restaurant

The inspiration for this recipe actually goes back to my childhood. My dad and I often went fishing. We'd head out to the lake with friends and family, and my dad would patiently teach me how to set up my rod and we'd sit. And we'd sit. As a child, I was a terrible fisher. I couldn't toss the line, I couldn't manage the bait and I most certainly couldn't sit still for more than 2 minutes. After what seemed like an eternity to a seven-year-old, I decided to give up. I wedged my rod into the rocks and took off to go play.

A little while later, I heard my dad yelling at me from the water. "Joe! Come back! You caught a fish!" I was ecstatic. I had caught a fish! I could fish. I was actually a little disappointed that I hadn't been there for the big moment. But it definitely renewed my interest in fishing with my dad. That's why at the restaurant this fish arrives at your table whole—from the head to the tail.

Years later, when I was a teenager, my dad told me the truth: he had caught the fish. I was a little crushed. But looking back now, I realize he had taught me a valuable lesson. Don't walk away from a challenge. And that's something I take into the kitchen with me every day. Recipes may not turn out, dishes may go wrong. But you have to keep trying because eventually you'll get it right. And you might discover you could do something you never thought you could.

> ½ cup kalamata olives (or olives of your choice),
> pitted and halved
>
> 2 baskets cherry (or grape) tomatoes
>
> 6 garlic cloves, halved
>
> 3 sprigs thyme
>
> 1 Tbsp olive oil
>
> pinch of salt and freshly ground pepper
>
> 2 lb (1 kg) sea bass fillets (or whole fish,
> cleaned and gutted)

Preheat barbecue to medium-high. Combine olives, tomatoes, garlic, thyme, olive oil, salt and pepper in medium bowl. Place into wire barbecuing basket or barbecuing tray (these containers have small perforations that allow the barbecue flavour into the food and are perfect for cooking smaller pieces of food on a barbecue).

Lay fish over tomato mixture. Sprinkle with salt and pepper. Cover loosely with foil. Cook on preheated barbecue for about 10 minutes until tomatoes are wilting. Turn fish over and cook for 3 to 5 minutes, depending on thickness of fillets, until tender.

Serves 6

Stjerneskud
(Danish Shooting Star)
Birgit Wildenhoff

Open-faced sandwiches are staples in Danish kitchens and Stjerneskud is one of the more elaborate of those. This recipe is for one, so just multiply with the number of guests.

Stjerneskud was a favourite of my husband's mother, an innkeeper in Denmark. There are a few variations of it, but I have tried to make it as close as I remember it. When we visited there many years ago from Canada, we brought our son-in-law to meet my husband's mother and he tasted this for the first time. To this day, he still fondly remembers her Stjerneskud and (no pun intended) gets stars in his eyes when talking about it.

FISH
- 2 small plaice (or sole) fillets
- all-purpose flour for dredging
- 1 large egg, lightly beaten
- ⅓ cup fine dry breadcrumbs
- canola oil for shallow frying

DRESSING

- 1 Tbsp mayonnaise
- 1 Tbsp sour cream
- 1 tsp finely chopped red onion
- 1½ tsp ketchup
- freshly ground pepper

SANDWICH

- 1 slice French bread
- butter
- 1 Boston (bibb) lettuce leaf
- 1 slice smoked salmon
- 3 large cooked shrimp, peeled and de-veined, leaving tails intact
- 3 asparagus spears, steamed
- 2 thin lemon slices
- 1 tomato slice
- 1 tsp caviar (such as salmon or lumpfish roe)
- 1 sprig dill

Dredge one piece of fish in flour. Dip in egg and then coat in breadcrumbs. Heat some canola oil in medium frying pan over medium. Cook fish for 2 to 3 minutes per side until golden brown. Remove to paper towel.

Roll up second piece of fish and secure with toothpick. Cook in small frying pan of simmering water (or white wine) for 3 to 4 minutes until just cooked; drain.

Mix all dressing ingredients in small bowl.

Toast bread and place on serving plate. Spread with a little butter. Place lettuce on bread. Top bread with both pieces of fish. Top with dressing. Arrange salmon, shrimp and asparagus on top of fish.

Twist lemon slices and arrange lemon and tomato on top. Top with caviar and dill.

Serves 1

Roasted Garlic Pasta

Duane Mercier

This recipe is a result of trying to recreate a dish served at a local restaurant (Linguini Sergio at Rigoletto's Café). I failed at recreating it, but created something new—well, new to me. It has become my staple pasta dish. To save time, I'll roast the garlic the night before (I like to use 6 bulbs—yes, 6 bulbs) and add either a chopped Cajun chicken breast or spicy Italian sausage to the pasta (garnished with a squeeze of fresh lemon). Or I'll substitute the basil and lemon for sun-dried tomatoes (half a small jar).

I feel very comfortable in the kitchen, so I do the lion's share of the cooking in our home. Hand me a bunch of ingredients and I will make it up as I go. Just don't ask me to bake—can't do that to save myself.

2 garlic bulbs
3 Tbsp olive oil, divided
3 Tbsp lemon juice
pinch of salt and freshly ground pepper

1 container cherry (or grape) tomatoes, halved
¾ cup chopped fresh basil
12 oz (340 g) penne (or bow tie) pasta

Preheat oven to 350° F (175° C). Remove excess papery outer coating from garlic bulbs. Place garlic bulb on small pieces of aluminum foil. Drizzle each with 1 Tbsp of oil. Wrap foil around garlic and place on baking sheet. Cook in preheated oven for 50 to 60 minutes until softened. Let cool.

Combine lemon juice, salt and pepper in small bowl. Squeeze out garlic from each clove into juice mixture; mash with fork.

Heat 1 Tbsp oil in large frying pan over medium-high. Add tomatoes, basil, garlic mixture, salt and pepper. Cook for about 5 minutes until tomatoes are hot and wilted. Stir in basil.

Meanwhile, cook pasta in large pot of boiling salted water for 12 to 15 minutes until *al dente* (firm but not crunchy). Drain and return to pot. Add tomato mixture. Stir to combine.

Serves 4 to 6

The Kids' Favourite Macaroni and Cheese

Amber Miller

My parents have cared for foster kids for a very long time; in fact, I was one of those kids at one point in my young life. For several years, I helped care for some of those kids with my now-husband. Three children in particular caught my love and attention, and they participated in our wedding in August 2009. The children have since been adopted. This recipe was one of their favourites. I consider it a legacy meal, something to remind me of our little makeshift family and the wonderful times we had together. It's something my husband and I will often make as we hope "our" children are doing well.

2 Tbsp olive oil

½ large red (or white) onion, finely chopped

3 Tbsp butter

3 Tbsp all-purpose flour

1½ cups milk

1½ cups cream (18% MF)

½ cup grated mozzarella (or provolone) cheese

½ cup grated Cheddar (or Asiago) cheese

1 cup chopped cooked ham

½ tsp paprika

pinch of salt and freshly ground pepper

2 cups cooked macaroni pasta

steamed green vegetables to serve (optional)

Preheat oven to 350° F (175° C). Grease medium casserole dish.

Heat olive oil in medium saucepan over medium. Add onion and cook for about 5 minutes, stirring occasionally, until softened.

Reduce heat to medium-low. Add butter and stir until melted. Stir in flour and cook for 1 minute. Slowly stir in milk and cream. Cook for 5 to 10 minutes, stirring occasionally, until thickened; remove from heat.

Combine both cheeses in small bowl. Add ⅔ cup of cheese mixture, ham, paprika, salt and pepper to milk mixture. Stir to combine. Stir in cooked pasta. Spoon into prepared dish. Sprinkle with remaining cheese. Bake, uncovered, in preheated oven for about 20 minutes until top is golden. Broil for about 2 minutes to brown top further if desired. Serve with vegetables if desired.

Serves 4

Salmon Pasta

Marg MacEachern

After hearing an article on CBC about the difficulty busy families have finding the time to prepare inexpensive, nutritious and quick meals, defaulting to the nearest fast food takeout, my husband and I decided to come up with something quick, cheap and easy. After a few minutes rummaging around the fridge and cupboard, we came up with these ingredients that in total cost less than $5. In 20 minutes this delicious, simple meal was ready to eat. We have eaten it many times since. Of course if you want to go over budget, you can pour a glass of dry white wine to complement the meal.

> **1 Tbsp olive oil**
> **2 garlic cloves, minced**
> **1 × 6½ oz (213 g) can wild red sockeye salmon, drained**
> **pinch of salt and freshly ground pepper**
> **12 oz (340 g) spaghetti**
> **1 cup finely grated fresh Parmesan cheese**
> **tossed salad to serve (optional)**

Heat olive oil and garlic in medium frying pan over medium. Cook for about 1 minute until fragrant. Remove and discard bones from salmon; add salmon to garlic. Cook for 3 to 4 minutes until hot, breaking up any large pieces of salmon. Add salt and pepper.

Meanwhile, cook spaghetti in large pot of boiling salted water for 12 to 15 minutes until *al dente* (firm but not crunchy). Drain. Add to salmon mixture. Add cheese and toss to combine. Serve with tossed salad if desired.

Serves 4 to 6

Garry's Pantry Pasta

Laurel Smith

This is my friend Garry's pasta recipe. Garry and I both served in the Air Force with the CF-18s in the late '90s and we were both deployed on a NATO tour of duty in Italy on different occasions. We always love to eat the local foods, and Garry said that when he went out to his favourite place he always ordered this pasta. On his return to Canada he started making this for his family to rave reviews. I watched over his shoulder the last time he made it and am very happy to share my friend's recipe. I love it because every good kitchen already has all of the ingredients in the fridge or pantry. It is also a great side dish or late-night snack.

12 oz (340 g) bow tie pasta (or your choice)
2 Tbsp olive oil, plus extra for drizzling
4 garlic cloves, minced
⅓ cup dry white wine
½ cup sliced sun-dried tomatoes in oil, drained

¼ cup hot banana peppers, sliced, plus 1 Tbsp of their juice
2 tsp capers, coarsely chopped
1 tsp dried crushed chilies
pinch of salt and freshly ground pepper
freshly grated Parmesan cheese

Cook pasta in large pot of boiling salted water for 12 to 15 minutes or until *al dente* (firm but not crunchy). Drain well; reserve about 3 Tbsp cooking water.

Meanwhile, heat 2 Tbsp of olive oil and garlic in large frying pan over medium. Cook for 1 minute until fragrant.

Add wine and cook for 2 to 3 minutes until reduced by half. Add tomatoes, banana peppers and their juice, capers, chilies, salt and pepper. Cook for about 5 minutes until hot. Add pasta and reserved cooking water and toss to coat.

Spoon onto warmed serving platter. Drizzle with extra olive oil and sprinkle with Parmesan cheese.

Serves 4 to 6

Betty Faulder's Creamy Mac and Cheese

Liane Faulder, food columnist for CBC Radio's
Radio Active *and the* Edmonton Journal

This was comfort food in our home. Nothing made me and my little brothers happier on a winter's night than a bubbling CorningWare casserole of elbow macaroni and good old Cheddar cheese sauce. Now my own grown sons often request this same dish when they come for dinner. My mom always took a dry crust of bread and tore it into little pieces and put those on, too, because the toasted bread adds a nice crunch.

➤ **3 Tbsp butter**
3 Tbsp all-purpose flour
pinch of salt and freshly ground pepper
3 cups milk (3.25% MF)
3¾ cups grated old Cheddar cheese, divided
3–4 cups penne (bow tie or elbow) pasta

Preheat oven to 350° F (175° C).

Melt butter in medium saucepan over medium. Add flour and stir for 1 minute. Add salt and pepper. Gradually whisk in milk. Cook for about 5 minutes, stirring occasionally, until thickened. Remove from heat; let stand for 3 minutes. Stir in 3 cups of cheese.

While sauce is cooking, cook pasta in large pot of boiling, salted water for 12 to 15 minutes until *al dente* (firm but not crunchy); drain. Return pasta to same pot. Add cheese sauce and stir to combine.

Spoon pasta mixture into medium casserole dish. Sprinkle with extra cheese. Bake in preheated oven, uncovered, for 10 to 15 minutes until hot and bubbly around edges.

Serves 6 to 8

Connolly's Easy Pizza Dough

Mark Connolly, host, CBC News Edmonton

Sunday night is pizza night in our house. I usually cook two pizzas, and the boys (Patrick and Jack) call it as "Dad's Pizza." My wife had this recipe in her cookbook when we got married 22 years ago, but I have changed it up a bit as I've worked with it over the years. I added some whole-wheat flour, which makes it a little healthier and gives some heft to the crust. I like it crispy rather than doughy, so I discovered that it helps to put it in the oven for five minutes or so before putting on the toppings. Don't put on too much cheese either, because that affects how quickly the dough cooks.

> **1½ cups warm water**
> **1½ Tbsp olive oil**
> **1 Tbsp dried instant yeast**
> **3 cups all-purpose flour, divided**
> **1½ tsp salt**
> **1 cup whole-wheat flour**
> **favourite pizza toppings, such as tomato sauce, cheese, seasonings and pepperoni**

Combine water and olive oil in small bowl. Combine yeast, 1 cup all-purpose flour, salt and whole-wheat flour in large bowl. Add water mixture. Mix to a sticky dough. Turn dough onto lightly floured surface. Gradually add enough of remaining flour to form soft dough. Knead dough for 5 to 10 minutes until smooth. Place in greased bowl; cover. Let stand in warm place for about 1 hour until dough has doubled in size.

Preheat oven to 475° F (245° C). Punch dough down. Lightly knead. Divide dough in half. Roll out to form 10-inch (25 cm) rounds. Place on 2 pizza pans. Bake in preheated oven for 5 to 7 minutes until edges start to turn golden brown. Remove from oven. Add favourite pizza toppings. Return to oven. Bake for 12 to 14 minutes until crust is browned and crisp and cheese is melted.

Makes 2

Smoky Sweet International Pizza

Jonathan Iverson

I put this pizza recipe together for the Italian Centre Shop, where I work. It was designed to highlight Voetbalkaas (football cheese), a Gouda made by a Dutch company specially for the 2010 World Cup. However, like that soccer competition and the Italian Centre itself, the pizza brings together a host of nations.

My clearest memory of the 2010 World Cup is the morning the Italian Centre stopped to watch the defending champion, Italy, be eliminated from the tournament. The players of the Azzurri, as the Italian team is known, were too old or too young and had struggled in the group stage. They had to beat Slovakia in the final game to guarantee staying in the competition. Through the morning, we could hear some cheers but mostly groans coming from the nearby café. Italy started poorly and went behind early in the game. They were trailing 2-0 in the second half when they woke up and halved the deficit. Then cheers in the Italian Centre turned to vehement cursing as an apparent Azzurri equalizer was ruled out for offside. A few minutes later, there was profound silence when Slovakia scored again, but Italy wouldn't allow its supporters the peace of abandoned hope, scoring in the 90th minute just to make it interesting. By the end of a thrilling match, the entire staff of the Italian Centre, from Italy and across Europe, Asia, Africa, South and North America, had gathered around one of the TVs on the floor, and all the customers were there shoulder to shoulder with us. The result did not crush all the viewers as, fitting with the Italian Centre's multi-ethnic dynamic, a handful of Slovakian supporters were among the staff and patrons. I soon shared the misery of the Italians as my English Lions were knocked out a few days later.

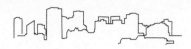

> 1 Tbsp sherry (or red-wine) vinegar
> 1 Tbsp olive oil
> pinch of granulated sugar
> ½ small red onion, thinly sliced
> ½ small red pepper, finely chopped
> 2 small (or 1 large) ciabatta bread loaves
> 8 oz (225 g) Gouda cheese (Dutch preferably), grated, divided
> 8 thin slices Black Forest ham
> pinch of smoked sea salt (optional)

Preheat oven to 400° F (205° C).

Combine vinegar, olive oil and sugar in small jar and shake well. Combine onion, red pepper and half of vinegar mixture in small bowl; set aside.

Cut bread in half lengthwise. Remove inside of bread, leaving crusty shell. (You can process the bread removed and make breadcrumbs for another use.)

Place bread shell, cut-side up, on baking sheet. Sprinkle with half of cheese. Add ham. Spread onion mixture over ham. Sprinkle with remaining cheese. Bake in preheated oven, uncovered, for 10 to 12 minutes until bread is browning and crisp and cheese is melted.

Drizzle with remaining vinegar mixture and sprinkle with salt if desired.

Makes 4

Zucchini Quiche

Vicki Giles

This recipe was given to me by my mum, who was given it by one of her friends. I loved it as a child, and my children are addicted to it, despite the fact that it contains zucchini. We usually eat the entire thing in one sitting. It is a great way to use up all the zucchini from the summer—we just grate it and freeze it in bags (measuring 3 cups per bag). Then, in the middle of winter, we can have a taste of summer by making this great quiche.

You can use a food processor to grate the zucchini, cheese and onion.

3 cups grated zucchini	½ tsp salt
1 cup grated white Cheddar cheese	½ tsp marjoram
½ cup grated onion	½ tsp oregano
4 large eggs, lightly beaten	¼ tsp cayenne pepper
1 cup all-purpose flour	¼ tsp freshly ground pepper
1 tsp baking powder	¼ tsp garlic powder
½ cup vegetable oil	½ cup finely grated fresh Parmesan cheese
1 Tbsp parsley flakes	

Preheat oven to 350° F (175° C). Grease 9 × 13 inch (23 × 33 cm) baking dish.

Combine all ingredients except for Parmesan cheese in large bowl. Spread mixture into prepared dish. Sprinkle with Parmesan cheese. Bake in preheated oven, uncovered, for about 45 minutes until set and golden brown. Let cool in pan slightly before cutting into pieces to serve.

Serves 4 to 6

Mixed Vegetable Stir-Fry

Kasim Kasim, Padmanadi Vegetarian Restaurant

When I grew up in Indonesia, my mother did all the cooking, and everything was vegan. The first thing I remember cooking by myself was a bean curd (tofu) roll, and I made my own bean curd, too. When I was 24, I opened my first restaurant in Jakarta, Indonesia, called Padmanadi. The name means "lotus waterspring." After my family moved to Canada, we opened up Padmanadi here in Edmonton in 2002. Ever since, it has been a place for us to make healthy, delicious vegan food. This mixed vegetable dish is one of my mother's recipes, and now it's on our menu.

A simple stir-fry is a great, tasty way to get more vegetables into your diet. In the summer, you can buy most of these ingredients locally at the farmers' markets in Edmonton. You can find dried radish in Asian grocery stores.

1 Tbsp dried radish

1 Tbsp vegetable oil

1 lb (500 g) green beans, cut into 1-inch (2.5 cm) pieces

1 medium green pepper, chopped

1 medium red pepper, chopped

1 medium orange pepper, chopped

2 medium carrots, peeled and diced

⅔ cup chopped vegetarian ham

2 Tbsp soy sauce

1 tsp granulated sugar

pinch of salt and freshly ground pepper

Soak radish in small bowl of boiling water for about 5 minutes to rehydrate; drain.

Heat wok over medium-high. Add vegetable oil. Add beans, green pepper, red pepper, orange pepper, carrots and ham. Stir-fry for 3 minutes until hot.

Add radish and remaining ingredients. Stir-fry for about 2 minutes until vegetables are tender-crisp.

Serves 4 to 6

No-Fail Pyrohy

Terry Sysak

I first learned how to make pyrohy when I was just 18 and a young bride. Since we were Catholic, we didn't eat meat on Fridays. I stopped by my aunt and uncle's store, saying I was going to make yet another tuna casserole this Friday. My aunt suggested pyrohy instead, but I didn't know how to make them. She came over in the afternoon, and let's be honest—she made them. She went out the back door just as my husband and uncle came in the front door, and they raved about these pyrohy. So I finally had to confess.

Since then, I've mastered our Friday night soul-food meal. Years later, another aunt told me about *her* no-fail recipe: just enough salt, just enough liquid and the secrets of the universe. It's the easiest one I've ever made.

Pyrohy used to be poor man's food, but now they've become a specialty dish. I serve these to my kids and grandkids and also to my non-Ukrainian friends. Everybody loves them. I've included my favourite potato and cottage cheese filling, but you can use whatever filling you like. This summer, I taught my 15-year-old grandson to make pyrohy, and now he makes them for his family. The tradition goes on.

DOUGH
- **4 cups all-purpose flour**
- **2 cups sour cream (14% MF), approximately**

FILLING
- **2 potatoes, peeled and quartered**
- **¼ cup butter**
- **1 small onion, finely chopped**
- **1 large egg, lightly beaten**
- **1 cup cottage cheese, drained**
- **pinch of salt and freshly ground pepper**

TO SERVE
- **vegetable oil (optional)**
- **1 Tbsp butter**
- **1 small onion, finely chopped**
- **pinch of salt**
- **sour cream (optional)**

Place flour in large bowl. Add enough sour cream to form soft dough. Knead until dough comes together. Cover and let stand for 1 hour.

To make filling, place potatoes in medium saucepan. Add enough water to cover. Simmer, uncovered, for about 15 minutes until tender. Drain well. Mash with potato masher. Stir vigorously with a fork to remove any large lumps. Spoon into medium bowl.

Melt butter in small frying pan over medium. Add onion and cook for about 5 minutes until softened. Add to potato. Add egg.

Put cottage cheese in small bowl. Using a fork or pastry blender, break down curds until fine and mostly smooth. Add to potato mixture with salt and pepper. Stir to combine.

To assemble, divide dough into quarters. Roll one quarter on lightly floured surface. Roll out to ⅛ inch (3 mm) thick. Using cookie cutter, cut 2½-inch (6 cm) circles.

Place 1 tsp of filling in centre of each circle of dough. Fold in half to enclose filling and pinch edges together to seal.

To freeze, put filled pyrohy on baking sheets; freeze. When frozen, transfer to sealable bags.

To cook fresh or frozen pyrohy, bring a large pot of salted water to a boil. Add a couple of tablespoons of vegetable oil if desired to stop pyrohy from sticking together. Gently drop pyrohy into water, stirring until water returns to a boil (to prevent them from sticking to bottom of pan). Cook for about 4 minutes, stirring occasionally, until hot and dough is cooked. Drain well.

To serve, melt butter in small frying pan over medium. Add onion and cook for about 5 minutes until softened. Transfer to large bowl. Add pyrohy and salt. Toss to coat. Serve with sour cream if desired.

Serves 4 to 6

Shahi Paneer
(Cheese Curds in Tomato Sauce)

Rajeev Bhasin, Khazana

I love people and I love food, so the restaurant business is perfect for me. I studied hotel management in New Delhi and worked in restaurants there, and I'm happy I was able to open up my own restaurant in Edmonton. Khazana means treasure, and we hope all of our customers appreciate the treasures of northern India that they can enjoy at our restaurant.

If you like Indian food, you've surely eaten butter chicken. Shahi Paneer is the vegetarian version—we simply use cottage cheese instead of chicken. *Shahi* means royal, and *paneer* is a soft, fresh cheese. It is a popular vegetarian dish from the northern region of India, eaten by the Mughal dynasty, which ruled India in the 17th and 18th centuries.

1 Tbsp butter

1 Tbsp canola oil

2 garlic cloves, minced

½ tsp finely grated fresh ginger

1½ tsp garam masala

1 tsp ground cumin

1 tsp dried fenugreek leaves

½ tsp cayenne pepper

1 × 14 oz (398 mL) can tomato purée

1 Tbsp chopped fresh cilantro

pinch of salt

pinch of sugar

4 oz (115 g) cubed firm curd cheese

2 Tbsp whipping cream

steamed rice to serve (optional)

Heat butter and canola oil in large frying pan over medium. Add garlic, ginger, garam masala, cumin, fenugreek leaves and cayenne pepper. Cook for about 1 minute until fragrant.

Add tomato purée, cilantro, salt and sugar. Bring to a boil. Reduce to a simmer. Cook for about 5 minutes until thickened slightly.

Add cheese and cream. Cook for 1 minute until hot. Serve over rice if desired.

Serves 2

Brunch & Treats

Potato and Beet Latkes

Mary Bailey, editor of The Tomato

Latkes are a traditional food in Eastern Europe, usually made by Jews during Hanukkah, the festival of light. I fondly remember the latkes that were served at the Hello Deli, a Jewish deli and an Edmonton institution in the 1970s and '80s. They had great chicken soup, too.

There are lots of different recipes out there for latkes, but I like to make mine with beets so that they look really pretty. They're delicious and a little bit different than a traditional latke. I usually make this recipe in the fall when the potatoes are at their best. These latkes are great for brunch because after frying them you can keep them in the oven to stay warm and they don't lose their crispness.

1 lb (500 g) russet potatoes, peeled
1 large beet, peeled and coarsely grated
1 medium onion, finely chopped
1 large egg, lightly beaten
2 Tbsp all-purpose flour

½ tsp baking powder
pinch of salt and freshly ground pepper
canola oil for shallow frying
sour cream for serving

Grate potatoes and place in fine metal sieve. Press as much liquid from potatoes as you can, or wrap in clean tea towel and squeeze excess water out.

Combine potatoes, beet, onion, egg, flour, baking powder, salt and pepper in medium bowl.

Heat enough canola oil to generously cover bottom of large frying pan over medium-high. Drop 2 to 3 Tbsp potato mixture into pan for each latke. Use back of spoon to flatten mixture so that each latke is about 3 inches (7.5 cm) in diameter. Cook for about 3 minutes per side until golden and crisp. Remove to paper towels to drain. Keep warm.

Add more canola oil to pan if necessary and heat before adding more potato mixture. Serve hot with sour cream.

Serves 4

Potato Pancakes

Olga Hancharuk, NorQuest College student

I came to Canada from Belarus in 2008 to join my husband. Though most people think of Ireland when they think of potatoes, many people in my country call Belarus potato country. Potato pancakes are almost a national meal, and I think everyone grows up knowing how to make them. This recipe was my favourite breakfast as a child. My mom and my grandmother would make it for me, and now I make it for my own family in Edmonton. It's a wonderful reminder of my country, my family and my childhood.

5 medium potatoes, peeled
1 large egg, lightly beaten
1 Tbsp all-purpose flour
pinch of salt
2–3 Tbsp vegetable oil
sour cream to serve (optional)
chopped cooked bacon to serve (optional)

Coarsely grate potatoes and place in colander. Press as much liquid from potatoes as you can, or wrap in clean tea towel and squeeze excess water out. Place in medium bowl. Add egg, flour and salt. Mix to combine.

Heat vegetable oil in large frying pan over medium. Carefully drop rounded tablespoons of mixture into pan, spreading them out a little using back of spoon. Cook for about 3 minutes per side until golden brown. Remove to paper towel–lined plate. Serve with sour cream and bacon if desired.

Serves 4

Gluten-Free Pancakes

Isabelle Gallant, CBC Edmonton

My dad's cooking was all about pleasure. His favourite things were fresh seafood and steak, and he fried his fish in bacon fat because it tasted good. Mom was the one who made sure we were eating healthy foods. My sister and I accompanied her on trips to the health food store, where she ladled natural peanut butter into plastic containers. I remember snacks of GORP (Good Old Raisins and Peanuts) and ants on a log, and there was never chips or pop in our cupboards.

I remember meals from both my parents on the weekends. Sometimes it was my dad's super brunch: perfectly soft scrambled eggs, crisp bacon, fluffy biscuits. Sometimes my mom made pancakes. She often used a recipe that included whole-wheat flour, cornmeal and wheat germ. I have to admit they turned me into a pancake snob. I loved their heartiness and their crunch, and as a result I've never been able to appreciate the fluffy white Bisquick version.

I've been experimenting with pancakes since last summer, when I discovered I have celiac disease. This means I can no longer eat gluten, a protein found in wheat, barley, rye and some other grains. Adjusting what I cook and creating a gluten-free kitchen has been one of the easiest parts of the process. There are so many wonderful, naturally gluten-free foods that I rarely feel like I'm missing out. My love of baking has not diminished, and I've discovered an excellent gluten-free flour blend that works almost like wheat flour in most recipes. There are so many resources out there now for the gluten-free cook that I'm never at a loss.

These pancakes are extremely flexible—I've made them with all kinds of different flour combinations, and they seem impossible to get wrong.

> ½ cup millet (or amaranth) flour
>
> ⅓ cup fine cornmeal
>
> ¼ cup flax seed meal
>
> ¼ cup tapioca starch
>
> 2 Tbsp sweet rice flour
>
> 2 tsp baking powder
>
> 1 tsp xanthan gum
>
> 1 Tbsp granulated sugar
>
> 1 tsp salt
>
> 2 large eggs
>
> 1 cup milk (3.25% MF) or soy milk, approximately
>
> ¼ cup melted butter (or vegetable oil), cooled
>
> extra butter for greasing

Combine millet flour, cornmeal, flax, tapioca, rice flour, baking powder, xanthan gum, sugar and salt in medium bowl.

Whisk salt, eggs, milk and butter in small bowl. Add to flour mixture. Mix to a smooth batter and whisk to remove any lumps. Let stand for 15 minutes.

Heat frying pan or griddle over medium. Grease with a little butter. Spoon small ladles (about ¼ cup) of mixture into hot pan. Cook for about 2 minutes until bubbles form on surface. Carefully flip and cook for 1 to 2 minutes. Keep warm. Repeat with remaining mixture, greasing pan before each pancake.

Makes about 6

Oat and Fruit Breakfast Mix
Eric Bishop

When I was a boy in England, I often went camping with the Scouts, and our breakfast usually included porridge followed by eggs and bacon or beans. If we were lucky, we occasionally had Corn Flakes, which we could not burn. Now I eat this recipe every morning. At age 78, I feel extremely healthy, which wasn't always the case. With this recipe, I use organic ingredients. The mixture can be made in advance and is ideal to take with you when hiking or camping. My wife and I just celebrated our 50th anniversary and we are doing everything we can to keep healthy. I feel fit and Jean still looks like a young lady.

> **1 cup old-fashioned oats**
> **2 Tbsp sunflower seed kernels**
> **2 Tbsp sliced almonds**
> **2 Tbsp medium coconut**
> **1 cup water**
> **pinch of salt**
> **1 cup stewed apple (or mashed banana or berries)**

Place oats, sunflower seeds, almonds and coconut in small food processor or coffee grinder. Process until mixture resembles powder.

Combine about ⅓ cup of mixture in small saucepan. Stir in water and salt. Bring to a boil over medium-high. Cook for about 3 minutes, stirring, until thickened and cooked.

Add apples. Stir until combined.

Serves 1 to 2

Old-Fashioned Bread Pudding

Marie Middleton

Bread pudding dates back centuries. It was invented to use up stale bread, and variations include both sweet and savoury puddings. This bread pudding recipe is one that I have made over the years, so I've been able to play with the recipe a bit. I usually substitute cut-up apples for the raisins. Five minutes before the pudding comes out of the oven, I'll spread strawberry or raspberry jam over the top. That's just enough time to melt the jam. When served, it will get a finishing touch of cream or ice cream to preserve the old-fashioned taste while adding a touch of sweet.

> **4 cups coarse breadcrumbs**
> **2 cups milk**
> **¼ cup melted butter**
> **½ cup granulated sugar**
> **2 large eggs**
> **1 tsp ground cinnamon**
> **¼ tsp salt**
> **½ cup raisins (or chopped apple)**
> **⅓ cup strawberry (or raspberry) jam**
> **whipping cream or ice cream for serving (optional)**

Preheat oven to 350° F (175° C). Place breadcrumbs in medium casserole dish.

Heat milk in small saucepan until bubbles form around side. Stir in butter; remove from heat and let cool.

Add sugar, eggs, cinnamon and salt. Whisk to combine. Whisk into milk mixture. Pour over breadcrumbs. Sprinkle with raisins. Bake in preheated oven, uncovered, for 45 minutes until almost set.

Spread with jam. Return to oven. Bake for 5 minutes more until set. Serve with whipping cream or ice cream if desired.

Serves 6

Johnny Cake Breakfast Parfaits

Lynne Kaluzniak

I grew up the baby of a family of seven children. My mom gardened, canned and made her own bread to feed all of us. We ate very organically, although at the time I remember thinking that we were deprived since the other kids at school brought sandwiches with store-bought bread and cookies. Ours were always homemade.

My mom made Johnny Cake on a regular basis. The recipe was handed down to her from her mom, who was Irish. She ate it in a most civilized way: sliced in half and covered in butter and honey. My dad invented the parfaits to amuse us children. He broke the cake up into a tall glass, covered it in milk and Rogers Golden Syrup, which was our favorite syrup of all. We used it on pancakes and even on cottage cheese!

Mealtimes were noisy and chaotic and full of talk and political discussion. My father's family (Bevington) was instrumental in getting the NDP going in Alberta. We always sat down together as a family, with the place at the end of the table beside my mom reserved for the "baby." I remember graduating from that spot to a spot at the side of the kitchen table with great pride. To this day, I love cooking and I owe that to my mom. I have continued her tradition of having my own family sit down every night together for supper.

> ½ cup butter, softened
> ½ cup granulated sugar
> 2 large eggs
> 2 cups all-purpose flour
> 1 cup cornmeal
> 5 tsp baking powder
> ½ tsp salt
> ¼ tsp baking soda
> 2 cups milk (3.25% MF), divided
> ½ cup golden syrup

Preheat oven to 425° F (220° C). Grease 9-inch (23 cm) square cake pan. Line base and sides with parchment paper.

Beat butter and sugar in medium bowl using electric mixer until smooth and creamy. Add eggs one at a time, beating well between each addition.

Combine flour, cornmeal, baking powder, salt and baking soda in medium bowl. Add to butter mixture alternatively with 1½ cups milk. Pour into prepared pan. Bake for 25 to 30 minutes until a skewer inserted in centre comes out clean. Let stand in pan for 10 minutes before turning onto wire rack to cool completely.

Cut cake into 6 equal pieces. Break each piece into bite-sized pieces and place in parfait glass or glass of your choice. Repeat with remaining cake. Pour remaining milk into glasses. Let stand for 5 minutes. Drizzle with golden syrup.

Serves 6

Toscapullat
(Tosca Buns)
Kaisa Tekoniemi

I grew up in Finland. After I finished school when I was 19 years old, I moved to Canada, leaving my family behind. I went to Ottawa to help my cousin because his wife was diagnosed with cancer and they had a new daughter.

My intent was to stay for six months and then return home, but I ended up staying in Canada forever. I moved to Montreal two-and-a-half years later and met my husband (also a Finn), and our daughter and son were born there. In the '50s and '60s, Montreal boasted a strong Finnish community of about 5,000.

We moved to Edmonton in 1969. There were only about 200 people connected with the city's Finnish society at the time. Keeping my culture has always been extremely important to me, and I've returned to Finland many times. In fact, I took both of my son's children to visit Finland, Sweden and Estonia. I waited until each grandchild turned 12 before taking him or her on this Nordic country tour.

These Tosca buns were my grandmother's favourite coffee cakes, and Mom made them whenever Mummi came visiting us. I passed the recipe along to my daughter. As a young girl, she had a sweet tooth and really enjoyed baking. Now she's a pretty good cook and makes these buns for me whenever I visit her home in Airdrie.

1¾ cups milk

1 package (2¼ tsp) dried yeast

2 Tbsp granulated sugar

½ cup butter

3¼ cups all-purpose flour, approximately

FILLING

¼ cup butter, softened

2 Tbsp granulated sugar

TOPPING

¼ cup butter

3 Tbsp granulated sugar

1 tsp all-purpose flour

1 Tbsp milk

1 cup sliced almonds

Heat milk in small saucepan over medium until bubbles form around edges. Remove from heat. Cool slightly. Stir in yeast and sugar. Let stand for 5 minutes until frothy.

Rub butter into flour until mixture resembles fine crumbs. Add yeast mixture and stir. Turn onto lightly floured surface. Knead until smooth dough is formed. Roll dough to form an 8 inch (20 cm) square, ¼ inch (6 mm) thick.

Grease 8 holes of ⅓ cup muffin pan. Spread softened butter over dough. Sprinkle with sugar. Roll up dough to form log. Cut into 1-inch (2.5 cm) sections. Place, cut-side down, into prepared pan; cover. Let rise in warm place for 45 minutes until dough has almost doubled in size.

Preheat oven to 350° F (175 °C). Bake buns for 15 minutes.

Melt butter in small saucepan over medium. Add sugar, flour and milk. Bring to a boil. Remove from heat. Stir in almonds. Divide topping between buns. Return to oven. Bake for 15 minutes until golden. Let cool for 10 minutes in pan before turning onto wire rack.

Makes 8

Marmalade Pudding with Custard

Teresa Bosse

I acquired this recipe 20 years ago on a trip to Britain with my husband. The Canadian bar celebrated its 100th anniversary in London, and after the festivities, we went to Scotland and wound our way through incredible moors and fields of heather, and thought the short ferry to the Isle of Skye would be romantic. We booked a night at a bed and breakfast in a centuries-old stone farmhouse, and asked the owners for a dinner recommendation. It turned out their daughter worked down the road at the Three Chimneys Restaurant in another of the ancient stone buildings on the tiny island. We enjoyed one of the most memorable meals we have ever eaten, featuring wild salmon and roasted pheasant. The highlight was dessert—marmalade pudding served with a simple custard sauce. I asked for the recipe and was thrilled that our server (the daughter) was able to convince the chef to comply.

At Christmas, I decided to try it instead of the traditional plum pudding. Well, that started our new tradition of having not one but two types of pudding at Christmas. And without fail it is the marmalade pudding that is always eaten up to the last crumb. The original recipe called for self-rising flour and used weights rather than measures, so I have modified it to Canadian measures and ingredients.

I make it ahead of time. It can be cooked and kept in the refrigerator for a day or two. It can also be cooked and frozen. Heat before serving by either re-steaming or using the microwave. You can also flame the pudding with some warmed brandy.

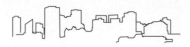

MARMALADE PUDDING

8 slices whole-wheat bread, torn
½ cup packed brown sugar
¼ cup all-purpose flour
½ tsp baking powder
½ tsp baking soda
½ cup butter
½ cup marmalade
3 large eggs

CUSTARD

2 cups milk (3.25% MF)
4 large egg yolks
⅓ cup granulated sugar
1 tsp vanilla extract
pinch of salt

Grease 4–6 cup (1–1½ quart/1–1½ L) heatproof pudding bowl. Place bread in food processor. Process until fine crumbs form. Combine breadcrumbs, sugar, flour, baking powder and baking soda in medium bowl.

Place butter and marmalade in small saucepan. Stir over medium until melted. Add marmalade mixture to crumb mixture and stir.

Beat eggs in medium bowl until light and fluffy. Fold into crumb mixture. Pour mixture into prepared bowl. Cover with buttered foil and secure foil with a string. Carefully place bowl into large pot. Add enough hot water to come halfway up side of bowl. Cover pot. Steam in gently simmering water for 1½ hours, replenishing water when needed, until pudding is cooked.

To make custard, heat milk in medium saucepan until bubbles form around sides. Whisk eggs, sugar, vanilla and salt in medium bowl until well combined. Slowly whisk in heated milk. Return mixture to same pan. Stir constantly over low for about 10 minutes until mixture coats back of spoon. Serve custard warm or cold, with warm pudding.

Serves 6

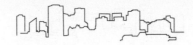

My Mother's Strawberry Soufflé

Anne Huennemeyer

This recipe has always made a way for my family to connect. My mother used to make it as a traditional dessert for my older sister's birthday—my sister was the lucky one who was born during strawberry season, and we *never* bought strawberries out of season. When I was little it was my job to help with the preparations. So, every year for as long as I can remember, my mother and I made this recipe for my sister. Now, years later, this recipe has become a favourite for my stepchildren. My stepdaughter, Ella, helps me make this dessert the way I used to help my own mother, and that is very special to me.

This soufflé also reminds me of the early years with my stepchildren. My stepson, Isaac, was at a stage when he did not eat any fruit or veggies unless they were puréed. I remembered this recipe—and man, was it a hit! My stepchildren were reluctant at first, not knowing the dish, but they loved it after they gave it a try. It was one of these early moments when we connected, and I believe it laid most of the groundwork for the rest of our relationship. When we visited my parents in Germany, my mother made it for us as her all-time favourite dish. In a way, this recipe has woven together my little patchwork family.

Even at 80 years of age, my mother is still a truly wonderful chef. I even call Germany from Edmonton when I need directions in the kitchen today. And now I look forward to the soon-to-come day when Ella will be her own master in the kitchen and I can ask her for advice.

➤ **¼ cup water**
1 Tbsp gelatin
1 lb (500 g) fresh strawberries, hulled
½ cup granulated sugar
1 cup whipping cream
½ cup strawberry yogurt
12 strawberries, halved, for decoration

| **Place** water in small saucepan. Sprinkle gelatin over water. Let stand for 3 minutes. Stir over medium until gelatin completely dissolves.

Place strawberries and sugar in blender or food processor and blend or process until smooth. Push through fine-mesh strainer, reserving purée in medium bowl. Discard seeds. Add gelatin mixture. Cover and chill for at least 2 hours until set.

Blend or process set strawberry mixture. Whip cream in medium bowl until soft peaks form. Fold in strawberry mixture and yogurt. Spoon into 6 to 8 serving glasses. Cover and chill for at least 2 hours or overnight if time permits.

Top with remaining strawberries and serve.

Serves 6 to 8

Wunderbar Old-Time Rhubarb Pudding

Bonnie Walter

Grandma was an old-country Volga German. She never measured anything, but knew how to eyeball the precise amounts. My mother figured out the recipe by watching. The fat in this dish was originally *any* kind of real animal fat they happened to have on hand in the farm kitchen (chicken, goose, pig, cow). (Warning: margarine or shortening will not do.) Rhubarb was the first fruit plant they had available in the spring in rural Saskatchewan. It's the best rhubarb pudding I've ever tasted—a family spring tradition. The almond extract is a luxury; you could use vanilla or nothing at all in a pinch.

5 large rhubarb stalks
⅓ cup butter, softened
¾ cup granulated sugar
½ tsp almond (or vanilla) extract
1 large egg

1 cup all-purpose flour
2 tsp baking powder
pinch of salt
½ cup milk
whipping cream to serve (optional)

Preheat oven to 350° F (175° C). Grease and line base and sides of 8-inch (20 cm) square pan. Remove any stringy bits from rhubarb. Cut rhubarb into ½-inch (1 cm) pieces; set aside.

Beat butter and sugar in medium bowl using electric mixer until light and creamy. Add almond extract and egg; beat well.

Combine flour, baking powder and salt in medium bowl. Add to butter mixture alternately with milk. Stir until combined. Stir in rhubarb.

Spoon into prepared pan. Bake in preheated oven for 30 to 35 minutes until skewer inserted in centre comes out clean. Let stand in pan for 10 minutes before cutting. Serve with whipping cream if desired.

Serves 6 to 8

Mun Cookies
(Poppy Seed Cookies)
Lawrence Bliss, Bliss Baked Goods

When I was growing up in Edmonton, we received a big box of sweets every year from my grandmother in Winnipeg for the Jewish festival Purim. The Purim tradition of sending food to family and friends is called *mishloach manot*, which literally means "sending of portions." Our Purim box from my grandmother always included these Mun Cookies (*mun* is the Yiddish word for poppy seeds). They are basic shortbread cookies with poppy seeds, cut into moon shapes because of how similar the word *mun* is to moon.

At home, I feel like I've been making these cookies for forever. But after starting the bakery 10 years ago, I started making these cookies as a reminder of my childhood. In our 495 square feet of space, this cookie has become a wonderful tribute to my grandmother and mother, who are no longer here to make them.

You can leave out the poppy seeds for a simple shortbread cookie.

2 cups butter, softened
1⅓ cups granulated sugar
3 large eggs
1 Tbsp vanilla extract

4 cups all-purpose flour,
   plus extra for dusting
½ tsp salt
½ cup poppy seeds

Preheat oven to 350° F (175° C). Grease 2 baking sheets.

Using electric mixer, mix butter and sugar in large bowl until creamy. Add eggs 1 at a time, beating well between each addition. Add remaining ingredients. Stir to combine.

Sprinkle a little flour on work surface. Roll out dough to ¼ inch (6 mm) thick. Cut out crescent shapes using a glass or cookie cutter. Place 1 inch (2.5 cm) apart on prepared baking sheets. Bake in preheated oven for about 7 minutes until cooked. Let stand for 5 minutes before removing to wire rack to cool completely.

Makes about 50

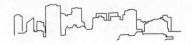

Lavender Crème Brûlée

Ivor MacKay, CBC IT and Red Seal Chef

This is a recipe I developed for CBC Edmonton as part of a series called "The 100-Mile Diet." The 100-mile diet simply means eating locally: if it's grown or raised more than 100 miles (160 km) from where you live, you don't eat it. I grew up with the diet in Nova Scotia. My family had a garden that produced our vegetables for the whole year. My father would partner with local farmers to buy local beef and pork—and yes, he helped with the butchering.

In June 2007, I challenged myself and my wife Lona (and my three teenagers somewhat) to eat local for one year. And to do it in Edmonton, where the growing season is pretty short. That meant cooking differently and spending a lot of time planning meals and preserving produce that wouldn't be available in the coldest months of the year. It also meant giving up foods that were not available within 100 miles (goodbye, coffee). We connected to the local farmers' markets and producers, met our challenge and lost some weight along the way.

Although we are officially off the diet, we remain committed to eating locally, and have turned our attention to our own backyard—we're getting dirt under our fingernails as we plant and harvest as much as we can.

- **2 cups whipping cream**
- **¼ cup alfalfa honey (or whatever type of honey you have in your cupboard)**
- **5 small lavender sprigs**
- **4 large egg yolks**
- **¼ cup superfine sugar (or dandelion honey)**

| **Preheat** oven to 325° F (160° C).

Combine cream, honey and lavender in medium saucepan over medium until bubbles form around edges.

Beat egg yolks in medium bowl using electric mixer until pale and thick.

Strain cream mixture. Add to egg yolks, stirring constantly. Place bowl over small saucepan of simmering water. Stir for about 8 minutes until mixture thickens and coats back of spoon. Pour into 6 shallow ramekins.

Place ramekins in roasting pan. Fill roasting pan with hot water until it comes halfway up side of ramekins. Bake in preheated oven for 40 to 45 minutes until just set. Let stand in pan to cool a little before removing. Cover and refrigerate for 8 hours or overnight.

Sprinkle each ramekin with sugar. Use small blowtorch to caramelize tops or broil for 1 minute. You can omit this step and instead drizzle ramekins with honey.

Serves 6

Back of the Yak Carrot Cake

Laurie Phipps-Campbell

I love moist carrot cake.

I mean, I really, really love moist carrot cake.

I began a quest for the best carrot cake recipe by asking friends, family and colleagues. I tried every recipe that came my way, but after two years, I still had not found The One. Then, finally, the Holy Grail of carrot cake recipes landed in my oven mitts. This divine dessert came from a woman I worked with, who got it from her friend, who got it from her aunt's mother's second cousin.

It made its debut at my next dinner party and didn't disappoint. It was to die for. As my guests enjoyed the cake's perfection, I explained the circuitous route to success. That's when my best friend declared, "OMG, that's a long route to this table." Her husband quipped, "Yeah, it travelled on the back of the yak." So, the lovely moist carrot cake was dubbed from that day forth "Back of the Yak Carrot Cake." Since then, it has been called to service many times at the Phipps-Campbell house.

- 2 cups all-purpose flour
- 2 tsp baking powder
- 2 tsp cinnamon
- 1½ tsp baking soda
- 1 tsp salt
- 1 cup granulated sugar
- 1 cup vegetable oil
- 4 large eggs
- 2 cups grated carrot
- 1½ cups grated peeled apple
- 1 cup golden raisins
- ½ cup chopped walnuts

CREAM CHEESE FROSTING

- 1 × 8 oz (225 g) package cream cheese, softened
- ¼ cup butter, softened
- 1½ cups icing sugar
- ½ tsp vanilla extract

Preheat oven to 350° F (175° C). Grease and line 9 × 13 inch (23 × 33 cm) baking pan.

Sift flour, baking powder, cinnamon, baking soda and salt into medium bowl.

Beat sugar, vegetable oil and eggs in large bowl. Add flour mixture. Add remaining ingredients. Stir until combined. Pour into prepared pan. Bake for about 50 minutes until skewer inserted into centre of cake comes out clean. Let stand in pan for 30 minutes before turning out onto wire rack to cool completely.

To make cream cheese frosting, beat cream cheese and butter until smooth and creamy. Beat in icing sugar and vanilla until well combined. Frost cake once it has cooled.

Serves 12

Bløtkake
(Norwegian Layer Cake with Whipped Cream Filling)

Ingrid Zukiwski

I was born in 1944 on Dyrøy Island in Norway, about 300 km north of the Arctic Circle. It was one of many islands that formed the county of Troms. Deep fjords and fishing made life unique and challenging. My parents wanted their five children to have a different future, so for economic reasons, they immigrated to Canada when I was eight years old. We crossed the Atlantic and joined our relatives in northern Alberta. A small mixed farm in the La Glace area, just 50 km northwest of Grande Prairie, became our home. When I look back at my mother's life, I'm sure the move was a culture shock. She didn't speak English, money was tight and both she and my father missed the saltwater fish that had been such a mainstay of their previous life. Yet she was positive, and that's a memory that has stayed with me.

Our family moved to Grande Prairie after my father suffered a stroke. In this city, we discovered many different nationalities. When I married my Ukrainian husband, I had a new culture to adopt. I learned Ukrainian cooking from my mother-in-law and our three children enrolled in Ukrainian dancing.

Still, preserving and maintaining my Norwegian culture is important to me. Cooking is one way I honour my heritage. For special occasions in Norway, Bløtkake is *the* cake to serve. This was the cake my parents served at their wedding in 1942. My brother and his Scandinavian bride kept up the tradition by having five of these cakes baked for their 80 guests. I bake this cake at least four times a year.

FILLING

- 2 lbs (1 kg) dried apricots
- 1 tsp salt
- 1 cup granulated sugar
- 1 quart (1 L) whipping cream

CAKE

- 10 large eggs, separated
- 2 tsp cream of tartar
- 2 cups granulated sugar, divided
- ½ cup cold water
- 2 cups all-purpose flour
- 2 tsp vanilla extract
- 1 tsp lemon extract
- 1 tsp salt

Preheat oven to 325° F (160° C). Combine apricots, salt and enough water to cover them in ovenproof dish. Cook, covered, for 1 to 1½ hours, stirring occasionally, until apricots are very tender and broken down. Stir in sugar; let cool completely. This step can be done a day ahead.

Whip cream and fold through completely cooled apricot mixture; chill until ready to use.

Preheat oven to 325° F (160° C). Line two 10-inch (25 cm) springform pans with parchment paper but do not grease. Beat egg whites in large, clean bowl until frothy. Add cream of tartar. Beat until soft peaks form. Add ½ cup sugar 2 Tbsp at a time, beating after each addition, until stiff peaks form.

In separate bowl, beat egg yolks, water and 1½ cup sugar until thick and pale.

Fold in remaining ingredients. Fold in egg white mixture in two batches. Separate cake mixture into prepared pans. Tap lightly on counter to remove any large air bubbles.

Bake for about 50 minutes until skewer inserted into centre comes out clean. Let stand in pans for 10 minutes before turning out onto wire racks to cool completely.

To assemble, cut both cakes in half horizontally. Place bottom of cake on serving platter. Top with some apricot filling. Place cake layer over top. Spread some more apricot filling over cake. Repeat with remaining cakes and apricot filling, and then cover entire cake with filling mixture.

Serves 10 to 12

Carrot Pumpkin Zucchini Cake

Dinu Philip Alex

I really believe that necessity is the mother of all inventions. When I moved to Canada in 2004 to do my graduate degree at the University of Alberta, I needed to cook to survive! I think that is where my passion for creative food started, and over the years it's evolved into a passion for fusion cooking—bringing the best of both the east and the west together.

I'm always watching the Food Network and one of my favourite shows is *Chopped*—a show where contestants are asked to make a dish out of ingredients that don't normally go well together. This is where I found my inspiration for the various ingredients in this Carrot Pumpkin Zucchini Cake. I have a sweet tooth, so I thought that if I could incorporate healthy ingredients into some of the sweet dishes I love, I'd be eating healthy while enjoying my favourite foods.

Try topping this cake with your favourite icing, garnished with dark chocolate shavings and a fresh mint leaf.

3 large eggs, separated

1 packet carrot cake mix (or carrot cake prepared from scratch)

2 tsp ground cinnamon

¾ cup milk (3.25% MF)

1 × 14 oz (398 mL) can pure pumpkin pie mix

1 medium zucchini, grated

½ cup vegetable oil

1¼ cups walnuts, toasted and chopped

2 Tbsp Canadian whiskey

Preheat oven to 350° F (175° C). Grease two 9-inch (23 cm) round cake pans or two 12-hole muffin pans.

Beat egg whites in medium bowl using electric mixer until soft peaks form. Combine remaining ingredients in large bowl. Fold in egg whites.

Divide batter evenly into prepared pans. Bake for 30 to 35 minutes for cake (or 18 to 22 minutes for muffins) until skewer inserted into centre comes out clean. Let stand in pans for 10 minutes before turning onto wire rack to cool completely.

Makes 2 cakes or 24 muffins

Cyflaith
(Welsh Molasses Toffee)
Barb Sinn and Bob Griffith

Our mom and grandmother made this each Christmas and for special occasions during the year (as did many other Welsh families). We have tried different brands of ingredients and fine-tuned the method as we make toffee or cyflaith for the Welsh pavilion at Heritage Days each year. Our mom would never have cut the cyflaith into squares or timed the boiling, but then again her mother never would have cooked it on an electric stove or used an electric fridge, so we don't feel that we are violating tradition with our modifications. Note that on hot, humid summer days, the toffee won't harden properly.

½ cup margarine

2 cups packed brown sugar

1 Tbsp water

1 cup fancy molasses

¾ tsp white vinegar

½ tsp lemon extract (optional)

Grease 9 × 13 inch (23 × 33 cm) baking pan.

Heat margarine, sugar and water in medium, heavy-based saucepan over medium until margarine melts and sugar dissolves. Stir in molasses. Cook, stirring, for 10 minutes. Remove from heat. Add remaining ingredients; be careful because mixture can splatter. Return to heat and cook for 10 minutes until candy thermometer reaches 305° F (150° C).

Immediately pour into prepared pan. To make nice little squares, refrigerate for 15 minutes. Then, using straight-edged utensil, mark grid of squares in toffee, starting with outside edges since they cool first. You may need to re-cut since molten toffee tends to swallow up the cuts. Or, leave pan to cool and set on counter. Once toffee is hard, break into pieces by smashing with meat mallet or rolling pin. Store squares or pieces in sealed container in cool, dry place.

Makes 24 squares or many small pieces

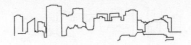

Wonderpoeding from South Africa

Miensie Kloppers

The Radio Active *crew—Rod Kurtz and Mark Scholz—made this dessert live on the air using the one-pot cooking method. The Kloppers heard about the plan and sent CBC the original recipe and some pointers. The pudding was cooked and consumed in 45 minutes.*

This recipe was sent to us from South Africa by my sister, Una McLachlan, in Christmas 1962. At that time we were living in the attic of an old house in Frankfurt, Germany, where my husband was studying. We were as poor as church mice and cooking on a one-plate stove. My mother had sent us a Presto Cooker so we could at least make soups and stews. This recipe was too good to be true: it could be made in the pot on our little one-plate burner!

This recipe serves 12, but the first night we made it, we devoured half in one go. It is rich and sweet—a family favourite. We have never tried to cook it over a campfire, but I am sure it could be done. Eventually we started baking it in the oven.

> - **3 cups all-purpose flour**
> - **½ cup granulated sugar**
> - **½ tsp salt**
> - **1 tsp ground cinnamon**
> - **1 tsp ground ginger**
> - **½ tsp ground cloves**
> - **½ cup softened butter**
> - **½ cup chopped toasted walnuts (optional)**
> - **2 tsp baking soda**
> - **½ cup milk (3.25%)**
> - **1 cup apricot jam**
> - **1 tsp white vinegar**
> - **whipping cream for serving (optional)**

Syrup

➤ 2 quarts (2 L) water
4 cups granulated sugar
2 tsp vanilla extract
½ tsp salt

| Preheat oven to 325° F (160° C). Grease 2 deep 8 × 12 inch (20 × 30 cm) ovenproof dishes.

Combine flour, sugar, salt, cinnamon, ginger and cloves in large bowl. Rub in butter until mixture resembles coarse crumbs. Stir in walnuts if desired.

Combine baking soda and milk in small bowl. Add to flour mixture with jam and vinegar. Stir until soft, sticky dough forms; set aside.

To make syrup, combine all ingredients in large saucepan over medium. Stir until sugar is dissolved. Increase heat to high. Bring to a boil. Boil for 5 to 7 minutes until thickened slightly.

Divide syrup between prepared dishes. Drop spoonfuls of dough in single layer into hot syrup. Cover with foil and bake in preheated oven for 30 minutes. Remove foil and continue baking for about 30 minutes until golden brown on top.

Cool before serving. Serve with whipping cream if desired.

Serves 12

Lemon Sugar Cookies
Heather Teghtmeyer

Every Christmas my mom would make a huge amount of goodies—tarts, squares, chocolates, you name it. She did all the baking herself with the exception of one treat—sugar cookies. In early December, my three sisters and I would roll up our sleeves, grab our rolling pins, flour and cookie cutters and spend the day baking and icing cookies.

As the years passed and we got older, Mom started to bake less and less, but without fail we would always make the sugar cookies. Even after leaving home, we still set aside a day to bake together. When my sisters had daughters, the number of helping hands in the kitchen simply increased. When I become a mother, I too will carry on the tradition of baking sugar cookies each holiday season…with my mom.

You can double the recipe to use the whole can of the sweetened condensed milk if preferred.

½ cup butter (or margarine), softened

½ cup granulated sugar

1 large egg

½ × 12 oz (340 g) can sweetened
   condensed milk

2 Tbsp lemon juice

1 tsp vanilla extract

2¼ cups all-purpose flour

2 tsp baking powder

½ tsp salt

FROSTING

2 large egg whites

⅛ tsp cream of tartar

⅛ tsp vanilla extract

1¾ cups icing sugar

food colouring (optional)

Beat butter and sugar in medium bowl using electric mixer until well combined. Add egg and beat until mixed. Beat in milk, lemon juice and vanilla.

Combine flour, baking powder and salt in medium bowl. Add to butter mixture; mix until dough is soft. Wrap dough in plastic wrap. Refrigerate for 1 to 2 hours until firm.

Preheat oven to 350° F (175° C). Grease 2 baking sheets.

Roll out dough onto lightly floured surface. Use desired shapes to cut cookies out. Place on prepared baking sheets about 1 inch (2.5 cm) apart. Bake for 8 to 12 minutes until lightly golden around edges. Cool on baking sheets for 5 minutes before removing to wire rack to cool.

To make frosting, beat egg whites, cream of tartar and vanilla in medium bowl until foamy. Add icing sugar and beat until stiff. Divide frosting between custard cups and tint with food colouring. Spread frosting onto cookies.

Makes about 24

Welsh Cakes

Jennifer Smith

It was 1967 and Margo Oliver's *Weekend Magazine Cookbook* was a constant in our mother's kitchen. But it wasn't a Margo Oliver recipe that my mother cooked most frequently from the cookbook; instead, it was her own handwritten Welsh Cakes recipe transferred to the protective custody of the inside cover of the cookbook. It had been lovingly transcribed from a timeworn, multi-edited, shortening-shined recipe card.

Ten years had passed since my mother, Morwen Smith's (née Jenkins), at 29 years of age, had tucked her recipes carefully into a trunk destined for the trans-Atlantic voyage from Liverpool to Montreal. The young Welsh family was moving to Canada.

Our family—my parents, my father's mother (our Gran), my sister and myself—embraced our new country. Being young children when we immigrated, my sister and I rapidly lost our foreign accents. Just as quickly, our memory of home as cliffs with a misty sea was displaced by images of grain elevators, golden wheat and prairie skies.

To my mother, however, becoming Canadian did not preclude following traditions of our heritage. On Sundays, supper was inevitably an English tea, and English tea in our home always included Welsh Cakes. By maintaining the tradition, we children began to realize that although we were Canadian, there was an Other that we belonged to. We had a cultural heritage too. We were Welsh.

The grandchildren in our now-extended family have taken their contribution to making Welsh Cakes very seriously. It is always the children's job to sprinkle sugar on the warm cakes. With the publication of this recipe, I hope that many more generations of children, Welsh or not, will have a teaspoon by the sugar bowl at the ready in eager anticipation of their responsibility. As the first batch of Welsh cakes appears, the children will sprinkle sugar over the warm little cakes, which is followed by an age-old involuntary action. Checking that the adult's attention is averted, a warm little cake will vanish, leaving a sugar trail around the mouth that somehow, magically, is never detected!

> **3 cups all-purpose flour**
> **1½ tsp baking soda**
> **½ tsp baking powder**
> **½ tsp salt**
> **1 cup shortening**
> **1 cup granulated sugar, plus extra for sprinkling**
> **1 cup currants, rinsed and patted dry**
> **1 tsp ground nutmeg**
> **2 large eggs, lightly beaten**
> **⅓ cup milk (3.25% MF), approximately**

Sift flour, baking soda, baking powder and salt into large bowl. Rub in shortening until mixture resembles coarse crumbs.

Add sugar, currants and nutmeg. Stir to combine.

Add eggs and enough milk to make soft dough. Wrap dough in plastic wrap and refrigerate for 15 minutes.

Roll dough out on lightly floured surface to ¼ inch (6 mm) thickness. Cut into 2-inch (5 cm) rounds using round, lightly floured pastry cutter.

Heat greased griddle, cast-iron skillet or electric frying pan to medium-low. Cook cakes for about 5 minutes on each side until golden brown. Transfer to wire rack. Sprinkle with extra sugar while still hot.

Serves 4

Torta 3 Leches

Nury Mora

I grew up in Venezuela and moved to Edmonton 9 years ago. I miss the hot weather and the food, so every time my mom comes to visit, I make her cook my favourite recipes. One Christmas, my mom came with my sister and grandma to visit me and my daughter. My grandma loved the snow, especially how it accumulated on the roofs of the houses. She said it looked like the movies, and she dreamed of making a snowman.

That visit, my grandma made this cake. My Venezuelan and Canadian friends tried it and loved it. After my grandma returned home, one of my friends asked me to get the recipe. I did and tried it out before passing it along—it tasted exactly like my grandma's cake. But for some reason, my friend hasn't been able to get the same flavour. So, once in a while she asks me to make it for her!

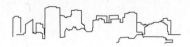

SAUCE

- 7 large eggs, separated
- 1¼ cups granulated sugar
- 1 Tbsp vanilla extract
- 1 Tbsp dark rum
- 1½ cups all-purpose flour
- 1 Tbsp baking powder

- 2 cups milk (2% MF)
- 1 × 12 oz (340 g) can sweetened condensed milk
- 1 × 14 oz (398 mL) can evaporated milk
- 2½ Tbsp dark rum
- 1 Tbsp vanilla extract

| **Preheat** oven to 350° F (175° C). Grease and line 9-inch (23 cm) round baking pan (you can use a springform pan but it can leak, so make sure you place it on a tray).

Beat egg whites in large, clean mixing bowl using electric mixer until soft peaks form. Gradually add sugar a little at a time until sugar dissolves. Add egg yolks one at a time, beating well after each addition. Add vanilla and rum.

Sift flour and baking powder into small bowl. Fold into egg mixture. Pour into prepared pan. Bake in preheated oven for about 40 minutes until skewer inserted in centre comes out clean.

Prick top of cake all over with skewer. Leave in pan to cool.

To make sauce, place remaining ingredients in medium saucepan over medium. Stir for about 5 minutes until well combined. Pour cooled sauce over cooled cake still in pan. Cover and refrigerate for 8 hours or overnight.

Serves 10 to 12

Jam Thumbprints:
Aunt Irene's Wartime Cookies

Deborah Anzinger, author of
Cook: You Can Cook Fast, Healthy Meals for Your Family

Aunt Irene was born in 1907 and passed away in her 99th year in 2006. She never had children due to a burst appendix as a young girl. She was young in the roaring '20s and filled my head with fantastic stories. Aunt Irene's wartime cookie recipe has always been a keeper. She gave it to me when I was feeling overwhelmed by the approaching holidays with two young children. She told me she first started making these cookies during the war when they did not have very many rations. She used the recipes for three different cookies: a raspberry jam thumbprint, a flattened cookie that was dipped in beaten egg and chopped pecans before baking and a plain cookie that she would mark with a cookie press. My children and family have always loved these simple cookies and ask for them throughout the year. I included Aunt Irene's cookie recipe in *Cook: You Can Cook Fast, Healthy Meals For Your Family* (first self-published, now soon to be published by Whitecap Books). It encourages movement back into the kitchen and getting the whole family involved.

- 2½ cups all-purpose flour
- ½ tsp cream of tartar
- ½ tsp baking soda
- ½ cup unsalted butter, softened
- ½ cup non-hydrogenated lard

- ½ cup granulated sugar
- ½ cup packed brown sugar
- 1 large egg
- 1 tsp vanilla extract
- ⅔ cup raspberry jam, approximately

Preheat oven to 350° F (175° C). Grease 2 baking sheets or line with parchment paper.

Combine flour, cream of tartar and baking soda in medium bowl.

Using electric mixer, beat butter, lard and both sugars in separate medium bowl until light and creamy. Add egg and vanilla and beat until well combined. Stir in flour mixture. Mix until well combined. Roll dough, about 1 Tbsp each, into balls. Place on prepared baking sheets about 1 inch (2.5 cm) apart. Press down gently in centre of each ball with your thumb to make indent.

Fill each indent with about ½–¾ tsp jam. Bake in preheated oven for about 12 minutes until lightly browned. Let stand on baking sheets for 5 minutes before removing to wire racks to cool. Repeat with remaining dough and jam.

Makes about 40 cookies

Sun Tea

Justine Jenkins-Crumb, Devonian Botanic Garden

I have been making sun tea since my daughter, now 14, was a toddler. It started out as a little project she and I could do together, but now I just love the simplicity of it. You take herbs from your own garden and leave them on the porch on a beautiful sunny day, and the sun itself makes the tea. It allows me to appreciate the sun and what it does for our world. It's truly organic.

To enjoy sun tea with fresh herbs from your garden, start prepping your ingredients in the dark days of winter. In February, start your seeds indoors for mint, thyme and lemon balm. Richters Catalogue is a great source for herb seeds. After the danger of frost is past, all new plants can go outside to acclimatize before you plant them. Herbs can be grown in flower or vegetable beds or in pots. Most herbs like sunny locations.

Lemon verbena can be successfully grown from cuttings—cut some new shoots in the middle of summer when all your weeding is done for the day, and stick them in moistened soil-free mix to root. Cuttings can be kept indoors in a sunny but not hot location over the winter. If lemon verbena and lemon balm are out of season, you can use lemon slices and some extra mint instead.

1 small handful lemon verbena, loosely packed

1 small handful mint leaves (apple mint preferably), loosely packed

8 sprigs thyme

1 small handful lemon balm

1 medium lemon, thinly sliced

2 Earl Grey teabags

2 quarts (2 L) water

Place all ingredients in jar. Place jar in warm, sunny place, such as on your front step. At sunset, take out teabags and discard. Strain tea into 2 quart (2 L) jar with screw-top lid or large jug with cover. Cover and chill for 8 hours or overnight. Serve over ice.

Makes 2 quarts (2 L)

Pam's Awesome Bannock

Pam Petrin, CBC *Radio's* Edmonton AM

My mom was the best bannock maker around. Of course anyone whose mom makes bannock would say the same thing. She was Cree, from Onoway, Alberta, and she passed away in 2008. I remember my mom's bannock fresh from the oven, piping hot. We'd smother fresh pieces with butter. It was the ultimate comfort food.

Whenever I asked Mom for her bannock recipe, she would just say, "Well…you throw in a little of this and a little of that," so it was pretty hard trying to make my own.

Last year I took a Cree language course and I wanted to make bannock for my classmates. Over many months I tried several different versions on my unsuspecting classmates. And even though this recipe is not quite what my mom's was, it is still quite delicious. Try it hot out of the oven and smothered in butter and/or some homemade jam. I like to add raisins or cranberries for something different, especially if I'm taking it camping. And speaking of camping, try using a bit more flour and wrap some of this mixture around smokies or hot dogs, then roast them slowly over a campfire…there's nothing like it.

> **4 cups all-purpose flour**
> **¼ cup granulated sugar**
> **3 Tbsp baking powder**
> **1 tsp salt**
> **2¾ cups water**
> **⅔ cup lard, melted**

Preheat oven to 350° F (175° C). Grease 9 × 13 inch (23 × 33 cm) baking pan.

Combine flour, sugar, baking powder and salt in large bowl. Make well in centre. Add water and lard. Stir with fork, adding a little more flour if needed, until mixture comes together. Place mixture in prepared pan. Bake for about 50 minutes until cooked and golden on bottom.

Serves 1

Index